Jack Mc.

GW01451634

# Look at it this way

DIFFERENT PERSPECTIVES ON CHRISTIAN LIVING

the columba press

First published in 2005 by
the columba press
55A Spruce Avenue, Stillorgan Industrial Park,
Blackrock, Co Dublin

Cover by Bill Bolger
Origination by The Columba Press
Printed in Ireland by ColourBooks Ltd, Dublin

ISBN 1 85607 494 3

# Table of Contents

# Introduction

In offering this book, I am only too aware that I am not offering something new or original. However, I dare to hope that I may offer a different perspective on something with which we are all familiar. The message of the gospels still stands, no matter how we choose to approach it. I have always tended to look for simpler and more direct ways of presenting it, in the hope that with understanding comes a greater response. I grew up with the belief that I lived my life, then I died and, depending on different factors, I ended up in hell, heaven, or purgatory. Many years later, I see things much more simply. I just hope this is 'wisdom' and not 'wishful thinking'. In this presentation, I am suggesting that Jesus was sent by the Father to catch up with us as we left the Garden, to tap us on the shoulder and to say, 'Come on back home. My Father is waiting to welcome you back, and to forgive everything. All you have to do is to turn to him with all your heart, and he will hold you close to his heart.' Jesus goes further, to tell us that he himself will lead us back to the Garden, as we would never be able to make our way by ourselves. We are then offered a supreme Gift, the Spirit and Breath of God, the Spirit of Truth and Power, who will enable us follow Jesus faithfully in all that he asks of us.

If we are heading back towards an eternal hug of forgiveness from the Father, it is only right that we should become 'huggers' along the way, ever growing in our willingness and capacity to forgive others at every step of the journey. Forgiveness must become a core expression of our love. We make this journey as a community, as a family, and we are nourished at the same table of the Eucharist. Each of us is uniquely endowed by God with the gifts he sees we need to fulfil our calling in life. The call can differ from person to person, and so will the gifts that are given to each. These gifts are called 'charisms', which means gifts that are given to us to be used in the service, and for the benefit of others.

The Way that Jesus points out to us is very definite, and I will never find myself in a situation in life where I am not sure which way to turn. The sign-posts are clear, and the gifts of wisdom, discernment, and knowledge are part of the tool box supplied for the journey. I refer to the cross as 'splinters', because many of us are seldom burdened with a very heavy cross. The splinters of daily living, all those many ways in which we have to die to self, make up the cross for most of us. Quite often this can be more demanding that one single cross, especially if it is one that attracts the sympathy and support of others. It's like comparing the funeral, when huge crowds are there in support, and then the loneliness that the bereaved experiences a few months later, when there's nobody around.

The titles of the chapters are deliberately intended to be evocative. Most of us are familiar with 'Broadband', where I speak about being 'on-line' to God, no matter what else I may be doing. Once again, referring back to an earlier part of my life, prayer tended to be compartmentalised; when I prayed I did nothing else, and when I worked, I did nothing else. I speak about landmines along the road, and many of us can identify with that image. Lead us not into temptation, but deliver us from evil. We can so easily take a false step and come to serious harm. I speak about pit-stops and, while writing this chapter, I was very conscious of having spent a few moments in hospital over the past summer. I have also benefited from Retreats, and times spent in a Hermitage I used visit back along the years. I re-emerged from such places with a real feeling of being 'topped up', and with a renewed sense of energy.

I have subtitled this book 'Different Perspectives on Christian Living'. None of the truths is new, of course, but it is my hope that I may be able to express them in a way that may make them easier to grasp. In the process of Revelation, something I read, something I see, something I hear goes a little bit towards lifting the veil and clarifying a truth. It is a life-long process that will not be completed this side of the Garden. It gives joy to my heart, though, when I think that I who write this, and you who read it, will all meet up again, as life was at the beginning of God's Creation, and we won't ever have to say goodbye again. Until then, my friend!

## Back to the Garden

God's plan of creation began in perfect harmony, and he saw that everything he created was good. As far as God is concerned that plan is still on offer, and what he creates and ordains continues to be good. The problem is not on God's side. Does God seem far away at times? Guess who moved?! Without going into detail about the nature of sin, and original sin in particular, suffice it to say that our human nature had to be brought back to the Maker, who alone could restore it to its original innocence. The computer I now use has had to be taken back to the factory on a few occasions, because there certainly was no way that I could or would attempt to repair it. On one occasion, the factory sent a technician to my home, and he did the repair work right here on the premises. I am bordering on the irreverent when I think of Jesus as being the technician sent by the Father to take on our human condition, set right all that had gone wrong, and then restore it to us in perfect working order. The problem is, of course, that the computer is basically still the same – keyboard, hard drive, software, etc. No matter what the technician did, if I don't have an anti-virus, or I insist on trying to make it do something for which it was never intended, then of course all the good work is wasted and I find myself in trouble again. I know my analogy limps a lot when I compare the redemption of human nature to the repair work of a computer technician, but it may help to grasp the core of what Jesus actually did.

Another way of looking at it is to think of Jesus undoing the damage, sorting out the mess we had got ourselves into, and inviting us to return to the Garden and begin all over again. In Gen 3:8, we are told that 'God walked in the Garden in the cool of the day'. Jesus invites us to return to God, and walk with him. In Lk 15:12, Jesus speaks of the Prodigal Son returning to the embrace of the Father, and recovering his inheritance. 'Come back to me with all your heart. Don't let fear keep us apart' are words we use in a song often used in Services of Reconciliation. Not only does Jesus invite us back to the Garden, but he himself offers to lead us there. In fact, he tells us that this is the only way we can get back. 'Nobody comes to the Father except through me' (Jn 14:6).

Let's look at this from another angle. I have just bought a new car, and I'm still enjoying the novelty! Supposing the car was stolen (perish the thought!). The car is recovered, and the person responsible for stealing it is brought into my presence. I just don't know how I would react, although I'm fairly sure I would not become violent or abusive, which would solve nothing. Let me switch back to the Garden again. What would/did God do when Adam and Eve rejected what he gave them, and opted for doing things their way? They wanted to assume God's power and position, something for which they had no right whatever, no more than the guy had who stole my car. God was prepared to forgive them. In fact, he offered them the very thing they had tried to assume to themselves. Still using the analogy of the car, he forgave them, offered them the car to keep, and included all the petrol they needed for the rest of their lives! He devised a plan, in Jesus, that would enable them to share fully in the life of the Divinity, and he also offered the Spirit (petrol?) that would enable them live with that Divinity for all eternity. No, indeed, that would not be our way of doing things!

It is important to remember that there is nothing automatic about God, either as Father, Jesus, or Spirit. Yes, indeed, Jesus did all that is needed for us to return to the Garden, and the onus is on us to accept the invitation, and to avail of the offer. God does not give me anything; he offers me everything. If Adam and Eve rejected God's plan, then of course we have to make a personal decision to accept it, and to go along with it. Remember, I speak of absolute pure free gift here. I cannot earn it, or merit it in any way, but I do have to accept it. Accepting the gift implies a whole new way of living, and a whole new way of seeing and thinking. Even that is pure gift. Every time I switch on the computer, my e-mail box is cluttered with junk mail, all offering me something that someone tells me I need. Many of these offers are free, in an effort to entice me into their web, and then the offers of items for sale come flooding in, if I accept the free gift. It is easy to 'fall' for these offers, and forget that there's a price tag lurking somewhere down the road. The only condition attaching to all and every offer from God is willingness on our part. 'Peace on earth to those of goodwill'(Lk 2:14).

The main problem, as I see it, is that my own brokenness is so close to me, is part of me, that I cannot see the wood for the trees. Faith is a response to love. I can accept in my head that Jesus did all he did for me, but my own personal experience of my human weakness prevents me from stepping out in faith, to do things, to see things, to believe things that I know are beyond my own personal ability. The fact of the matter is that they are beyond my ability. There is no way that Peter, of himself, could walk on water (Mt 14:29). However, when Jesus invited him to have a go, he stepped over the side of the boat! He managed very well until awareness of his own limitations hit him, and he took his eyes and his attention off Jesus. From that moment, he was in trouble. He became more aware of his own weakness, and lost sight of the power and strength of Jesus. 'Keep your eyes fixed on Jesus, the author and finisher of our faith' (Heb 12:2).

There is one point that must be emphasised here. With the gifts comes the Giver. In other words, I must totally accept Jesus as my Lord and Saviour, and then, and only then, am I able to receive all he has to give. Jesus himself is very much part of the package; indeed, he is the package, and all the graces of heaven's treasuries come with him. 'Having given us Christ Jesus, will the Father not surely give us everything else?' (Rom 8:17). I said earlier that Jesus invites us back to the Garden, but he insists that we follow him there. We could never get there on our own. The problem referred to in this paragraph is that I may be convinced about being saved, redeemed, freed from bondage, etc., and yet experience myself as very weak, broken, and sinful. That is the miracle of redemption. Grace builds on nature; it doesn't replace it. In actual practice, I still have my weaknesses to deal with, but I now have what I need to do so. While I live in the body, I'll have to struggle with the burdens and limitations that this places on me. If you ever waken up some morning, and discover that your life is exactly the way it should be, don't move; just wait for the undertaker! St Paul discovered something very important about his weaknesses. 'I was given a thorn in the flesh, a true messenger of Satan, to slap me in the face. Three times I prayed to the Lord that it leave me, but he answered "My grace is enough for you; my great strength is revealed in weakness" '(2 Cor 12:7-9). Paul goes on to say 'Gladly, then, will I boast of my weakness, that the strength of Christ may be mine … For when I am weak, then I am strong' (2 Cor 12:9-10).

Elsewhere we read Paul speaking about his personal experience of his weakness and brokenness. This is worth quoting in full, because it really gets to the core of the issue under reflection:

'We know that the Law is spiritual, but I am full of human weakness, sold as a slave to sin. I cannot explain what is happening to me, because I do not do what I want, but, on the contrary, the very things I hate. Well then, if I do the evil I do not want to do, I agree that the Law is good; but, in this case, I am not the one striving towards evil, but it is sin living in me. I know that nothing good lives in me, I mean, in my flesh. I can want to do what is right, but I cannot do it. In fact I do not do the good I want to do, but the evil I hate. Therefore, if I do what I do not want to do, I am not the one striving towards evil, but sin which is in me. I discover, then, this reality: though I wish to do something good, the evil within me asserts itself first. My inmost self agrees and rejoices with the law of God, but I notice in my body another law challenging the law of the spirit, and delivering me as a slave to the law of sin written within my members. Alas for me! Who will free me from this condition linked to death? Thank God! The answer is in Jesus Christ our Lord. He has set me free'(Rom 7:18-25).

I have quoted from Paul at some length, because he explains our predicament very well. At the end of the day, we are still weak human beings but, because of Jesus, we can come back to the Garden. St John tells us that there is a Spirit within us that is stronger than any evil spirit we may meet along the road of life (1 Jn 4:4). A wise old man was explaining to a group of young people about human nature. He told them that there are two large dogs within each human being, one is good, and the other is bad; and they are always fighting, and each is determined to win. One of his pupils asked him which of them normally wins the battle, and the old man replied, 'Always the one you feed the most.' If I make myself the beginning, or the centre of my atten- tion and reflection, I am doomed to failure. EGO may point to making myself the centre of my universe, but the letters could also stand for Edging God Out. In simple language, we do not have what it takes to make our way back to the Garden. The whole journey of redemption is, from beginning to end, the work of Jesus, a work that is brought to completion through the actions of the Spirit. Despite my weakness, my brokenness, and my sinful humanity, I keep throwing in my willingness; I keep repeating my 'Yes', and I *know* that the Spirit will do the rest. As I travel this road with Jesus, the Spirit, and Mary my mother, I actually become aware of some change happening within. Nothing very dramatic, but a deeper sense of peace, of sincerity, and of conviction that the process is working. While awareness of brokenness will always be there, I become aware of an ability to accept that 'shadow self', and know that Jesus is concentrat- ing on *all* of me. As my conviction of his love becomes more real and evident, I begin to realise that, warts and all, I can actually come back to the Garden. The Garden becomes that place of rec- onciliation between the Prodigal and the self-righteous brother; Martha and Mary, and the apostles who argued about who among themselves as to who was the greatest. The road back to the Garden is a way of forgiveness; it involves forgiving myself, those who have hurt me along the way; and it ends up with a full and eternal hug of forgiveness from the Father who is watching the horizon awaiting my return. There is a legend about the Day of Judgement. As the crowds flock in the gates of heaven, Jesus is seen standing outside, with his hand shading his eyes from the sun, as he stares off into the distance. Someone asks him what he is doing, and he replies, 'I'm waiting for Judas'. I know that I'll have to pick up on this theme of forgiveness in a later chapter, because it is central to becoming fully immersed in the Christian message.

# Popeye's Spinach

Only God can do a God-thing. The Father sent Jesus to complete the first part of our redemption. The weeds in the wheat (Mt 13:25-30) were not sown by the farmer, who had ensured that the seed was good. When God created us, he saw that we were good, and we *were* good (Gen 1:26). When the farm labourers asked the farmer where the weeds came from, he told them that 'an enemy has done this'. The word Satan means 'enemy'. The weeds of sin, sickness, and death were not part of God's creation. It was to remove these weeds that Jesus came. They had become part of us, and it was totally impossible for us to remove them by ourselves. Even if I could cut off a leg or an arm, my human weaknesses are still part of me, and, of myself, I cannot do a thing about them. Jesus came to take away the sins of the world; he came to heal the sick; and he completed his victory when he overcame death. As far as Jesus was concerned, his work was then completed.

When we speak of Jesus during the Mass, we use the past tense. By your cross and resurrection, you have set us free. Dying, you destroyed our death; rising, you restored our life. Before he died on the cross, Jesus cried out to the Father, 'It is accomplished', and then he bowed his head and died (Jn 19:30). He had completed the work his Father gave him to do. On many occasions he had told his followers that he had come with a mission, and that mission was to do what the Father asked him to do (Jn 6:38). He had now completed the mission entrusted to him. His next task was to convince his followers that he actually did overcome death. He spent forty days with them, appearing in the most unlikely places, and at the most unlikely times. He asked for something to eat, to let them see that he wasn't some sort of disembodied spirit; and he himself cooked a meal for them, because they had been fishing all night, and were bound to be hungry. These forty days were most precious, and very significant. It was the turning of the corner. He had come to the end of his journey, and was now free to turn around, and return to the Father. Once he did that, the Spirit would come upon us, so that we could begin the second part of the programme of redemption. When Jesus returned to the Father, he would pass on the baton to the Spirit, who would be entrusted with completing the work of Jesus, and direct our feet on the road that leads straight back to the Garden. St Paul tells us that there are two parts to our salvation – 'His blood and our faith' (Rom 3:25). 'His blood' obviously refers to what Jesus did, especially to his death on the cross. 'Our faith' must be understood very clearly and definitely.

At best, my faith could be little more than mental assent, knowing that Jesus is God. If I accept that as something that even Satan knows, I can hardly call it faith, if it is only in my head. Faith is in my heart, and it makes its way down into my feet. When it is translated into action, and becomes a direct response to what Jesus offers me, then I can call it faith. The origin, and the very source of our faith is the work and the gift of the Spirit. When my faith becomes the motivator for my stepping out, when it comes from my feet, rather than my head, then I am ready, willing, and able to respond to the offer of salvation, and to the invitation to return to the Garden.

I cannot overstress the simple basic fact that we speak of pure gift when we speak of faith, and any quality or quantity of faith. We are extraordinarily weak, because of the damaged nature we inherited through original sin. When Adam and Eve fell for the lie in the Garden, they came under new management. They hid because they were afraid (Gen 3:8). This is the first time 'fear' is spoken of in the Bible. Because the damage inflicted came from the father if lies, they were no longer able to tell the truth, or indeed to recognise the truth. Adam blamed Eve, and Eve blamed the devil and, in many ways, we tend to do a lot of that since. Jesus called the Spirit the Comforter, the Advocate, and most especially the Spirit of Truth. The Holy Spirit would be the antibody, the antidote, the antibiotic for the pollution of original sin, which was based entirely on a lie. When Jesus completed his part of the plan of salvation and redemption, it then would become the role of the Spirit to develop in us a spirit of truth, so that we could respond to the freedom that was offered us. 'From the Father, I will send you the Spirit of truth who comes from the Father. When this Helper comes, he will testify about me' (Jn 15:26). 'It is better for you that I go away, because as long as I do not leave, the Helper will not come to you; but I am going away, and then I will send him to you. When he comes he will uncover the lie of the world, and show clearly what its lie has been … I still have many things to tell you, but you cannot bear them now. When he, the Spirit of Truth, comes, he will guide you into the whole truth' (Jn 16:7-8, 12, 13). 'You will be my true disciples if you keep my word. You will know the truth and the truth will set you free' (Jn 8:31-32).

To summarise what exactly Jesus is saying here: I have cleared a way for you, back to the Garden. There will be many distractions along the way, as if the evil one keeps turning the sign-posts in different directions, to confuse you, and lead you astray. On your own, you would be like someone dropped into the thickest jungle, without compass, pathway, or weapon for hacking through the growth. The Spirit, and the Spirit alone, can direct your feet out of that jungle, and lead you directly to the Garden.

Let there be no doubt whatever about this. The first step in the process of our salvation was the decision of the Father to send Jesus. The second step was what Jesus did when he came. The third and final step is what we allow the Spirit to do in and through us, so that Jesus' work on earth may be completed. If the Father had not decided, in his love, that we should return to the Garden, he would not have devised the whole plan of redemption in the first place. If Jesus had not accepted his mission, in total submission to the Father's will, the road back to the

Garden would not have become available to us. If the Spirit did not come to complete the work of Jesus, we would never be able to find that road, or to stay on it, even if we did stumble across it. When Jesus passed the baton on to the Spirit, he also gave us that Spirit, so that we could walk in the light and the power of that same Spirit. The Spirit would do the work, and would enable us co-operate in the work of responding to the offer of redemption and salvation; this is not something we could possibly do by ourselves.

'That we should live no more for ourselves, but for him, he sent the Holy Spirit, as his first gift to those who believe, to complete his work on earth, and bring us the fullness of grace.' With tongue in cheek, I headed this chapter 'Popeye's Spinach'. I did so to emphasise that we need a Power greater than ourselves to respond to the gift of salvation. Lucifer, as well as Adam and Eve, were very 'God-blessed' ones. From much personal experience, they knew that God loved and cared for them. It is frightening to think that, even with all that, pride could still enter into the formula. Only God is perfect, and only that Mary, the Mother of Jesus, was so solidly grounded in humility and wasn't capable of considering herself superior to God, she too might well have bit the dust. She was so filled with the Spirit (of Truth), that she couldn't possibly see something that was not there, or claim something to herself that was not hers by right. She was unique in every sense of that word, and she was walking in the way of the Spirit long before Jesus had paid the price, or the Spirit was made available to the apostles, or to the early Christian community. She herself, of course, had never any doubt where all of this came from. 'He that is mighty has done great things for me, and holy is his name' (Lk 1:49). Humility is truth, and it is a solid-fountain humility when it acknowledges how truly blessed we are. The important point is to realise the source of that goodness. 'Lord, you are good and holy, and all that is good and holy comes from you' (Eucharistic Prayer II).

It is not possible to exaggerate how weak and frail our human nature is. God is the potter and we are the clay, the work

of his hands. The more beautiful, delicate, and ornamental pot-
tery the frailer it looks, even to the extent that one might be
afraid to take it in hand for fear of dropping it, or damaging it in
any way. To be perfectly honest, I would not be happy if God
made us 'unbreakable'! I believe that it's in the struggles and
tensions of life that the Spirit works best. All growth in my life
has always been in times of my inner human conflicts, temptations, and decisions of goodwill. There would be no value in
my 'Yes', if it made no difference whatever whether I said 'No'.
Good, by definition, will always be tested by evil, and the experience of my own weakness is the source of any compassion or
empathy I may have for my fellow-travellers on the road of life. I
am continually faced with choices, but the presence of the Spirit
can make it possible for me to make the correct choices. An alcoholic could be sober for thirty years and yet, with one drink, it all
comes unstuck, and the sobriety of the previous thirty years
counts for nothing. The disease is called alcoho*lism;* it never becomes alcohol*wasm*! To the day he dies, John will always be an
alcoholic, no matter how long his sobriety has been. Sin is like alcohol – cunning, baffling, powerful, and very very patient. One
unguarded moment and the whole good has turned to dust. The
breath of the Spirit is as necessary for my spiritual life, as air is
for the life of my body. I repeat something already stated in this
chapter: It is only through the presence and power of the Spirit
that I can respond to the redemption and salvation made available to me in Jesus. Through the whole plan and work of the
Trinity, I am directly depending on the Trinity to become part of
that plan. If Lucifer, or Adam and Eve, could fall from grace,
there's no reason to believe that I have any chance of avoiding
something similar.

   I am sitting in front of a computer as I write. There is a light
by the side of the computer, which is switched on, because the
room is in the basement and is usually quite dark. Whenever I
move away from the computer, for a cuppa or to go out on some
errand, I always ensure that I save what I have written. My ever-
present concern is a power-failure. I have learned of the reality

of such a thing through many unfortunate events over the years. One second of electric failure, and all my work for the past hour or so is wiped out. Once the power is cut off, everything comes to a standstill. I still have the computer, in good working order, and a light that has all parts in working order; except, of course, there is nothing running! The power is cut off, and everything has come to a standstill. I'm sure that, in time, all these electrical gadgets will have back-up batteries installed, which will kick in if the main power cuts out. For many hours at a time, I am not consciously aware of the electricity that I just take for granted. As I mentioned earlier, there have been times when this smugness led to a rude awaking. I use this analogy to illustrate the ever-presence of the Spirit within my being, even when I am not consciously aware of it. I have a card on the side of the computer which reads 'Holy Spirit, please help me'. I placed it there to remind me, and I must say that it does what it was intended to do. Jesus said that the Holy Spirit will 'remind you of all that I have said to you' (Jn 16:12-15). The Spirit will be the one who will teach us what we need to know, and who will lead us into all truth.

To live in the truth is to walk in the Way. It is when we become hostages to deceit, denial, and lies, that we follow the way that leads from the Garden, just as Adam and Eve had done. Part of the work of Satan is to disguise deceit and lies as the truth. Part of our sinful condition is that we can be blinded to it, and our rationalisation and self-justification can convince us of anything. Of myself, I have no reason to trust my own judgement because, even without being aware, I can be quite selective when it comes to truth. Only the Spirit of Truth can keep my feet on the way of truth. The Spirit is like an oculist, who can refocus my vision and enable me see what is really there. Jesus opened up the way back to the Garden, but it is only the Spirit who can lead me into that Way, and who can guide my feet into the way of peace. There is no way that I can ever hope to comprehend all Jesus did to effect my salvation, but even after all that, the whole process comes to nothing if I fail to allow the Spirit take over, and complete that work within me. What happened to Jesus happened in Israel. What the Spirit does is what happens in my heart, which becomes my own Holy Land.

# Tool Box

Life is a journey and, for the average person, it can be quite a long journey. I don't pretend to understand why one life should be for a minute, and another should be for a hundred years. This doesn't bother me, because I leave all such decisions to God, in the belief that he knows what he's doing. If he doesn't know what he's doing, there's little point in me trying to make sense out of it.

I have a strong preference for a journey by car, because I hate packing. It's great to be able to open the boot (trunk?), and throw in everything I think I might need. I usually end up with one piece of luggage (for appearance sake!), but walking gear, toiletries, medication, reading material, etc., are usually in their own small plastic bags. I am also past the stage where I feel that I must have everything I might possibly want, before leaving home. I have never gone to a place so undeveloped that there wasn't a shop or two where I could pick up a toothbrush, or a packet of antacid tablets. By and large, I take reasonable precautions, and this applies equally to the condition of the car, and a map or two, which are permanent features in the car anyhow. I drink quite a lot of water, and I always make sure that there's a bottle of water on the passenger seat, for a 'slug' now and then.

Why should I inflict you, gentle reader, with the unexciting details of my preparation for setting out on a journey? I began this chapter by referring to life being a journey; indeed, it is a journey that's made up of many many relatively short journeys. Referring to what I bring with me, I hope, will give me an opening to how I should approach life, and ensure that I have access to the more important and essential elements that make that journey fruitful, blessed, and empowered. I wrote at length in the last chapter of the central role of the Spirit in this journey. The Spirit accompanies me, as well as encouraging and empowering me. Christy Moore, the Irish singer/songwriter, has a song called 'Don't forget your shovel if you want to go to work.' This song came from his experience as a labourer in England in early life, where a shovel was the only tool required by most Irish navvies. This chapter could well be called 'Don't forget your tool box if you want to live today'. Most of us know someone who goes out the door to work in the morning, complete with all necessary equipment and data, including the car, which is supplied by the firm. The travelling technician has a tool box, with all the tools and material that will be required to do his work that day. He has a worksheet, and a mobile phone, again supplied by the firm, and his job is to go here, be there, fix this, change that. His employers have fully equipped him for this particular kind of work, and they even throw in a few refresher courses from time to time, to keep the workers up-to-date on all the latest developments.

As a Christian, I am entrusted with a life, and all that it takes to live that life to the full. 'I came that you should have life, and have it in abundance' (Jn 10:10). Jesus spoke about us having his joy (Jn 15:11), and his peace (Jn 14:27). In other words, with the responsibilities come the privileges. 'You will receive power from on high, and you will become my witnesses' (Acts 1:8). This is the most *extra-ordinary* situation that my mind could dare to imagine. I am given the gift of life, and I am given every gift and grace that I need to live that life to the full. Let's reflect on this for a while.

I take a copy and pen, and begin to write out all the things I'm good at. I list my hobbies, interests, and pastimes. I make a list of the significant people in my life, and the natural gifts and talents that are obvious to everybody, some of which may be directly connected to my particular profession, or vocation in life. I'm sure I could end up with several pages, by the time I have written down all that comes to mind. And yet, what I speak of here is away above and beyond all of that. It is wonderful to have natural talents, and I admire (envy?) those who are musicians, artists, and talented sports-people. However, when I speak of the tool box that is given me to live my Christian vocation, then all 'normal' ways of assessing and reckoning go out the door. The Spirit supplies a tool box of pure free gifts. These gifts are not mine; they are given to me for the sake of others. That, in itself, greatly increases my responsibility for how I use those gifts. Each person is completely unique, right down to a fingerprint, or a DNA blood sample. Because each person is so unique, it is only natural to expect that no two tool boxes will be the same. Some of my confrères are working with lepers, something I am certain would be beyond me. On the other hand, not many of them would dare sit at a computer for hours, trying to put words on reflections, thoughts, and ideas. My tool box contains exactly the tools that I need to do the work the Lord has entrusted to me. It is said that if there were one hundred people in a room, and they each exchanged their weaknesses, within an hour each would be screaming to be given their own weaknesses back! Something similar would result if you and I exchanged tool boxes. You have gifts that I don't need (e.g. you're a parent, and I am a priest), and I have gifts that you don't need. Gather a group of us in a large room, and each is entrusted with the gifts that God sees each one as needing. All of the gifts have one thing in common. They are not natural talents, or gifts of particular genius. They are charisms, from the Greek word *charismata*, meaning gifts given to persons for the sake of those they will meet along the road of life. In other words, while no one of us can claim a charism as personal property, each one of us can benefit from all the charisms in the whole room, and not just the ones entrusted to me. By the very fact that these charisms are common property, and never private possession, no one of us can claim any kind of superiority over anyone else. The Mother of Jesus was blessed in an extraordinary way by God, but there's no record of her working a miracle. I couldn't imagine her being jealous of the apostles because of the many miracles and signs that accompanied them in their post-Pentecost preaching! St

Paul was obviously a very powerful communicator, through the spoken and written word. I wouldn't feel it necessary to re-search his history, for proof that he raised anybody from the dead, or that he multiplied loaves and fishes.

I believe it would be a very worthwhile exercise to take time out (prayer?) to reflect on the particular tool box the Lord has entrusted to me. There is need for a word of caution here. I my-self would/should be the last person in the world to discover a particular gift of the Spirit entrusted to me. Of course, I can be aware of a gift, but this is revealed to me by others, and not through my own discovery. I have reason to believe that I have been entrusted with the gifts of preaching and teaching, and the reservations in my diary for over a year from now confirm this fact, rather than some great enlightenment on my part! There are many gifts, of course, that are common to all of us and, if I am being lead by the Spirit, I can expect to hunger for greater faith, or for greater wisdom. Remember my referring to a hundred of us gathered together in a large room. Imagine a very large mir-ror that is shattered, and one piece of the broken mirror is en-trusted to each person in the room. Each represents part of the whole, and it is only when each becomes willing to make avail-able the piece entrusted to their care that we can build a church, or form a Christian community. Each piece of the mirror repre-sents a different aspect of God, and it is only when all the pieces are reunited that we can hope to reflect the face of God. Jesus makes it very clear that each of us will be held accountable for what we did with the gifts entrusted to us (Mt 25:15-28). Everybody is gifted by God in a unique and special way. Those who are completely dependent on others, because of a physical or mental disability, contribute enormously to the Christian growth of those responsible for their welfare.

To be responsible is to respond to what God has entrusted to me. Like the technician going out the door to work in the morn-ing, I already have all that I'll need to live that day to the full. Each situation will require its own particular gift, and the Lord will never lead me into a situation where his Spirit will not be there to see me through. How unfortunate and foolhardly it would be to imagine that, of myself, I have all that's needed to meet each and every emergency this day may throw in my way. At this stage in my life, thank God, I am quite active, and I'm nearly always on the move. Should the time come when I find myself in a wheelchair, I can be sure and certain that I will have what it takes to deal with that situation. I don't have that gift just now, because I don't need it. To live each day with this level of faith is to live and to walk in the Spirit. It is by prayer, in whatever form that may take, that I am constantly reminded of this basic and simple truth. If I am too busy to pray, then I am far too busy. It's so easy for us to become so involved with the urgent that we overlook the important.

When I began this chapter, I prayed to the Spirit to anoint my words, and to make the gift of prophecy available to me. Prophecy is not about foretelling the future, as much as interpreting the present. I could not dare to speak God's word for him. I can make myself available, and trust a particular gift to guide and bless what I do. At every moment of every day, I can consciously allow the Spirit to work through me, either through the prayers I pray, the words I say, the things I do, or the very person that I am. Jean Vanier says that some of the greatest movements for good in the history of the world are brought about through the quiet prayers of totally unknown people.

One of my personal inspirations in my life is constantly reminding myself of Mary, my mother, as being the caretaker of my heart. It is my belief that she is particularly effective and active in reminding me of the basic truth about using the gifts, and living with the strength of the Spirit. Her whole life was a constant witness to this simple fact. I can imagine her whispering 'Yes' in each and every situation, whether on her way to Egypt, or to Calvary. She had no doubt whatever about the source of her strength, because 'He that is mighty has done wonderful things for me' (Lk 1:49). She was wonderfully endowed with all the gifts, and I just couldn't imagine her assuming any of these to herself, as her property or right. I think of it as highly significant that she should spend those waiting days with the apostles, until the Spirit came upon them. There was a separate tongue of fire for the head of each of them, and each was individually anointed and blessed. Not all wrote letters, nor did all face a martyr's death. Some of them are reputed to have travelled to far away countries to spread the good news, while some of them didn't wander too far away from Jerusalem. Each was lead by the Spirit to where the Lord required them to be.

In one of the most important documents that came out of Vatican II, *The Church in the Modern World,* we are told: 'All of the charisms of the Spirit are to be eagerly sought after by all of God's people, as being necessary and essential for the renewal of his Body, the church.' Yes, indeed, don't forget your tool box if you want to live today. With the call comes everything that is needed to answer that call. Place a Bible on your kitchen table as a reminder of your tool box; or carry a small edition of the New Testament on your person. Do anything and everything that will help to re-enforce in your heart something that is crucial and central to living the vocation to which you are called.

## Hugs on the Way

The road back to the Garden leads us into the eternal hug of the Father. The longest journey begins with the first step. The prize at the end of the road can be experienced within certain limitations during the journey itself. There is a big word called 'eschatology' and it has to do with the doctrine about death, judgement, hell, and heaven. Essentially it says that all that will be, is already here, although we have to wait till a later time to be able to comprehend it fully. In other words, I will only really understand these realities after I die, even though I know that they already exist. I mention this because I believe that the Father's hug is already available to us, even if we are very limited in our ability to comprehend the full implications of that truth. I would suggest that the nearest I can come to realising the fullness of this promise is that I accept that the forgiveness is mine and, because of that, I begin right now to share out that forgiveness to all those around me. To forgive is to remit, to let off when it involves a debt; or to pardon, when it involves an offence. Redemption is a word that comes from the time when slaves were bought and sold. Christian charities collected money and, when they had enough, they bought a slave from the slave-owner, and then allowed the slave go free. Redemption meant to free another from a bondage of any kind; and surely being trapped in slavery must be one of the worst forms of bondage. I have no rights, I have no possessions, no future, or no hope of bettering my human condition. To be redeemed by another is to be given a complete and absolute total free gift; something that, of myself, I could never hope to achieve. In cases when a slave escaped, he/she had to live the life of a fugitive, always looking over one's shoulders and never sure when the trap is going to spring, and life would end up much worse than before.

Inviting me back to the Garden is God's guarantee that total redemption and forgiveness awaits me there when I arrive. Because the end of my journey ends up in complete reconciliation with God, then my journey up to that point must display my own willingness to offer forgiveness and reconciliation to those I meet along that journey. Unconditional forgiveness is offered by God and, because I believe that this will be my certain destiny, I myself must use every opportunity life gives me to dispense forgiveness to each and every one who offends me. My journey towards my own complete forgiveness should be especially remarkable by my own willingness to forgive others along the way. Jesus tells a very interesting and significant story in the gospel. Because of what we can learn from it, it is worth quoting in full:

Then Peter came to Jesus and asked 'Lord, how often should I forgive someone who sins against me? Seven times?' 'No!' Jesus replied, 'seventy times seven. For this reason, the kingdom of heaven can be compared to a king who decided to bring his accounts up to date with servants who had borrowed money from him. In the process, one of his debtors was brought in who owed him millions of dollars. He couldn't pay, so the king ordered that he, his wife, his children, and everything he had be sold to pay the debt. But the man fell down before the king, and begged him 'Oh, sir, be patient with me, and I will pay it all.' Then the king was filled with pity for him, and he released him, and forgave his debt.

But when the man left the king, he went to a fellow servant who owed him a few thousand dollars. He grabbed him by the throat, and demanded instant payment. His fellow servant fell down before him, and begged for a little more time. 'Be patient, and I will pay it', he pleaded. But his creditor wouldn't wait. He had the man arrested and jailed until the debt could be paid in full.

When some of the other servants saw this they were very upset. They went to the king and told him what had happened. Then the king called in the man he had forgiven, and

HUGS ON THE WAY

said 'You evil servant! I forgave you that tremendous debt because you pleaded with me. Shouldn't you have mercy on your fellow servant, just as I had mercy on you?' Then the angry king sent the man to prison until he had paid every penny' (Mt 18:21-35).

Jesus concluded the parable with these words: 'That's what my heavenly Father will do to you, if you refuse to forgive your brothers and sisters from your heart.'

I have quoted this fully, because I consider it to point to the core of a very important Christian value. If I forgive, I am forgiven; if I don't forgive, I am not forgiven. On this journey of forgiveness, it would be a good idea to begin with myself. Guilt is not from God. Jesus says that he came to save the world, not to condemn it (Jn 12:47). Satan is called 'the accuser of our brothers … he accuses them before God night and day' (Rev 12:10). Having remorse, regret, sorrow, for what I have done is not guilt. I did what I did, and it can't be undone. 'O God, give me the serenity to accept the things I cannot change …' The only way to deal with my sins is to wash them away in the blood of the Lamb. It's like putting badly stained clothes into a washing-machine, with a very powerful detergent. The clothes come out the other end, completely cleaned and spotless. God wastes nothing. 'All things work together onto good, for those who love God' (Rom 8:28). The only value the past has are the lessons it taught me. Any compassion I may have has come out of my own experience of weakness and brokenness. I would be a much humbler, tolerant, and compassionate person today, if I learned everything life has taught me, especially through my own failures. '

A friend is someone to whom you may pour out all the contents of your heart, grain and chaff together, knowing that gentle hands will sift it, keep what is worth keeping and, with the breath of kindness, will blow the chaff away' (Arabian proverb). Jesus is such a friend. It is vital that I get real with him. He or his message is not just some nice idea that would make the world a better place, if taken seriously. No, I can turn to him right now,

and invite him into my heart, with a whip of chords, and ask
him to rid my heart of everything that is not of him. If I am sincere in what I'm doing, I stand up at the beginning of Mass, and
confess my sins, and ask for forgiveness. Should I then take all
those sins back out the door with me when I'm leaving?

There is such a thing, of course, as guilt. I can be found guilty
in a court of law, and receive a penalty for it. What I am speaking about here is what remains after the sins have been con-
fessed, the penalty is served, the contempt is purged. 'I continue
to flog myself' is a phrase often heard. The guilt involved here is
more self-condemnation, impatience with self, wounded pride,
than anything else. If I really want to become a forgiving person,
then I must begin with myself. In the catechism of my school
days, there was a teaching about some spot or mark being left,
even after a sin is forgiven. In other words, I'm forgiven, but not
really! God buries the hatchet, but he marks the spot, to dig it up
when needed. I know it's not possible for the human mind to
fully grasp the enormous generosity and scope of God's love.
When God forgives, he suffers from total amnesia, and forgets
all. Should I confess 'I did it again, Lord', he will be puzzled at
the 'again', because he has forgotten the last time. When God
forgives our sins, he dumps them in the deepest lake of his infinite mercy. Problem is, he puts a sign on the lake: 'No Fishing'.
God created us in his own image and likeness, and we can easily
return the compliment! 'Your God is too small' is the name of a
popular religious book of some years ago.

I could continue to the end of this book with this whole area
of forgiving myself, and how basic and essential it is, but I must
move on. Anyhow, it is only the Holy Spirit who can implant
this truth in the heart, and not the number of pages I use in writing about it. If I have any personal knowledge of Jesus, then I
surely couldn't have any problem accepting his readiness to forgive, and to ask me to do the same. 'I want you to love one another as I love you' (Jn 15:12). Loving one another includes
myself.

I personally believe that forgiveness is a gift of the Spirit, so my point of departure is to open my heart to the Spirit, and ask for the gift. Remember we are talking about 'seventy times seven' here; that is forgiveness for everybody. The road to heaven is heaven. On my way back to that eternal hug, I must begin dispensing my own hugs along the way. If I do this, I become more and more Christ-like and, when I do reach the Father, he may see much more family resemblance in me when he looks at me. Becoming a forgiving person involves a whole process of transformation. Transformation is prefaced by information and formation. The place to begin is the teaching of Jesus.

Read what he said, again and again, in many and different situations. In the one short prayer he taught us, he gives us the words 'Forgive us our sins, as we forgive those who have sinned against us' (Lk 11:4). 'If you forgive people's sins, they are forgiven; if you do not forgive, they are not forgiven' (Jn 20:23). The public sinner who washed Jesus' feet with her tears, was declared to be forgiven 'because she has loved much' (Lk 7:47). In other words, if this woman was alienated from God, she could not possibly love the way she does, because love comes from God. It is important to notice the scope for interchange here between love and forgiveness. The journey home is a journey of love that is expressed very powerfully through forgiveness. To err is human; to forgive is divine. I am walking the path of reconciliation, and that path leads safely back into the arms of my heavenly Father.

Once again, at the risk of being repetitious, I stress that this is only possible through the Spirit working within. I referred earlier to information, meaning following Jesus around in the different gospel situations, and seeing how he treated others. This information will filter from the head down into the heart, and the Spirit will use it to form my heart, and give me a forgiving heart. What extraordinary and powerful example is placed before me, to hear Jesus praying for those who are killing him, and offering eternal reconciliation to a wayward sinner on a cross beside him. How could I possibly not see forgiveness at the very core of his message, and deeply ingrained within his own heart?

'I came to save the world, not to condemn it' (Jn 3:17). God leaves all judgement to Judgement Day, and he asks us to do the same. If we are to continue his work on earth, then we have no choice but to try to live as Jesus lived. He wrote the script, and it's up to each of us to act our parts. It is a musical, and every discordant note will send shudders through the listeners. We are the leaven in the dough, and our presence is supposed to make a difference. Gordon Wilson from Enniskillen in Northern Ireland, was known worldwide for one thing: he publicly and repeatedly forgave those who had planted a bomb in a public place, which killed his daughter. The whole country was deeply moved by his example, and witness. Although he did not live in the Irish Republic, he was persuaded by the Dublin government to become a member of the Senate, and he did so till his death a few years ago. It was felt that his very presence, in the Senate, or anywhere, would be a powerful influence for good on those around him.

One of the paradoxes in the gospel is the stress put on the power available to the meek, the gentle, the forgiving. The world couldn't deal with Mahatma Ghandi, Martin Luther King, or Steve Biko. In refusing to strike back, they were seen to have a power greater than guns. The only way the world could deal with them was to kill them. Jesus was gentle, meek and humble of heart (Mt 11:29). He set out his stall in Bethlehem, and he showed how God views things. Pride is the greatest cause of unforgiveness, because there is something in us that needs to triumph over others, and we demand our pound of flesh, to satisfy our ego. When I refuse to let the ego run wild, and do the Christlike thing, I am slowly but surely moving along that road to the Garden. A straw shows the way the wind is blowing. I show the direction my life is taking through my actions. 'Seventy times seven.' Again and again and again. This must surely be *gift*, because, of myself, I never could do this. I'm not talking about being a doormat, and allowing others walk all over me. No, no. When necessary, Jesus took a very firm stand against the stubborn, obstinate Jewish religious leaders. He told them what he

thought of them, in no uncertain language. If, however, he de-
tected goodwill on their part, as with Nicodemus (Jn 3), he was
completely at their service. An apology is effective only when it
is accepted. Satan could not possibly repent, because his pride
would never allow him admit that he was wrong. The religious
leaders were so self-righteous as to be destructive in their intol-
erance of others. There was no forgiveness in those hearts,
which, like marble tomb stones, were filled with filth and rotting
bones. They could never become life-giving people. When I forgive another, I set that person free, but I also set myself free. It's
so easy to get caught in the trap of a resentment. Resentments
are very destructive, and are often a luxury most of us can ill afford. If I have a resentment against you, it's as if I'm drinking
poison, and I'm expecting you to die.

I feel I have only skimmed the surface of this whole area of
forgiveness and, as I continue to reflect, I see more and more
areas that need to be kissed with forgiveness. I will end this
chapter now, however, trusting the goodwill of you, gentle
reader, to take what is offered, and check out your own road
back to the Garden. I'm sure I have written enough to highlight
the absolute necessity of constant and on-going forgiveness
along the way, as I move nearer the greatest hug of forgiveness
that is possible, and am held in that hug for all eternity.

PS: 'But when you are praying, first forgive anyone you are
holding a grudge against, so that your Father in heaven will forgive your sins, too' (Mk 11:25).

# Food for the Journey

Some years ago, I travelled to Larne, in the north of Ireland, to say Mass for a prayer group. It was a dirty winter night and, as soon as the Mass was over, I was anxious to get on the road. While the group was singing the second verse of the closing hymn, I had removed the vestments, and was out the sacristy door. My car was parked near the entrance, facing Dublin! As I walked towards it, I heard somebody call out to me. I confess to my self-concern, and I refused to react, or to look back. As I got into the car, I looked in the rear-view mirror and saw an elderly lady struggling to catch up with me. She had a walking stick, which she had put under her arm, presuming she could move faster without it. With a groan of self-pity, I resigned myself to the inevitable, as I lowered the window. I was prepared to hear her life-story, and all the people in her life who were in need of prayer. When she caught up with me, she was out-of-breath with the effort. 'Father, I made these for you to be eating on your journey home.' As she said this, she produced a little boat-shaped wicker-basket, covered in cling-film. The basket contained the tastiest little triangular egg and onion sandwiches I have ever eaten. I was humbled and moved, as I pulled away. Many years later, that little basket is still here on my desk as I write and, when I become aware of it, I think of it as food for the journey.

On many occasions, I have made a connection between the significance of those sandwiches, and what has just happened when I come out of a church after Mass. Yes, indeed, Jesus provides us with food for the journey. When Moses led the Hebrews through the desert, the Lord let fall a bread from heaven, which covered the ground each morning. It was called manna, and what was available each morning was for that day only. Some of the people, with concern for tomorrow, saved some of it from one day, but the following day it was inedible. They were punished for not trusting God's care for them. Jesus taught us to pray for our daily bread. He called himself the bread of life, and he presented himself as life-giving food, giving a life that would be eternal. Obviously, on my way back to the Garden, I already have the sandwiches.

Eucharist ties in with so much of what Jesus is all about. On Calvary, he reversed the pollution of original sin with the antibiotic of his 'Yes' to the Father, completely neutralising the poison of the 'No' in the Garden. I was not present on that original Calvary, but the 'Yes" of then is repeated, and offered to the Father in every Mass, and I am offered an opportunity to add my 'Yes' to Jesus's 'Yes' to the Father. The chalice represents the death of Jesus. 'Father, if it's possible, let this chalice pass from me' (Lk 22:42).

Before I raise the chalice at the Offertory, I put a drop of water in the wine. In doing this, I am joining my 'Yes' to his. Where did the water come from? That is the water of my baptism. Water was poured on me back then, and someone else said a 'Yes' for me. Now I can do so myself, and I can do that every single day of my journey in life, as I head back to the Eternal Feast. Water represented both life and death for the Hebrews. Water was life-giving, especially in the barren desert, and yet it was water God used to defeat their enemies as they drowned in the Red Sea. Jesus turned water into wine, to show me what he can do with the one drop I offer him. He walked on water, to show that he had control over life and death.

For the Christian, death is like a pile of sand at the end of my life, which I can take, and sprinkle, a little at a time, as I journey along the road of life. For the Christian, death is what happens during my life-time. When was the last time you died for another? 'Greater love than this no one has, that a person should lay down a life for another' (Jn 15:13). I have to die to my selfishness, my greed, my pride, my arrogance, as I love, forgive, and reach out to others. It is in this dying that we enter into eternal life right now; we begin to live a quality of life that flows freely into the Sea of Love for eternity in heaven. We renew our commitment to this dying every time we share in Eucharist.

There is a beautiful story about the disciples on the road to Emmaus on Easter Sunday morning. They are on their way home (as they think), dejected, disappointed, and very crest-fallen. They had lived with a dream that had become a nightmare, and it was all too much for them. They had lost hope, which is the stabiliser of life and living. They were joined by Jesus as they walked along, but they failed to recognise him. He asked them the reason for their apparent depression, and they were amazed that he, or anyone else, did not actually know what had happened back in Jerusalem. They proceeded to tell him and, as they were finished, he proceeded to open their hearts to what actually did happen, and to make a connection between that and what the prophets of old had predicted would happen. It was all very interesting to them, but it was when they reached Emmaus that they finally came alert, opened their eyes, and recognised him. When he took a piece of bread, and offered to share it with them, they knew immediately that it was Jesus. The fact that they did not recognise him physically is understandable. The post-Easter Jesus takes on many colours and disguises, and is not always easy to recognise. He is now to be found 'where people are struggling for survival as human beings' *(Cry the Beloved City)*. I find it very moving to hear what the disciples had to say after Jesus left them. 'Were not our hearts burning within as he talked to us along the road, and explained the scriptures to us?' (Lk 24:32). What a beautiful journey. This is very similar to what I have in mind as I now reflect on the accompaniment of Jesus in our lives, as we travel home.

God could have loved us from a distance, but he chose not to. That is why and how Jesus can walk the way with us, and be the food and nourishment for the journey. He *is* our daily bread. The secret, of course, is to keep my 'Yes' within the day. I cannot live today on a 'Yes' I said yesterday. I open my heart as well as my mouth when I receive Eucharist. Like Mary visiting Elizabeth, I carry Jesus with me wherever I go. 'Lord, may your presence within me touch the hearts of those I meet today, either through the words I say, the prayers I pray, the life I live, or the very person that I am.' 'Having given us Christ Jesus, will the Father not surely give us everything else?' (1 Cor 1:5).

Bread figures largely in scripture. When the Hebrews wanted to fast, or to come boldly before their God, they ate unleavened bread, or bread without yeast, which was tasteless and unpleasant. 'No leavened bread is to be eaten' (Ex 13:3). 'Do not offer bread made with yeast when you sacrifice' (Ex 23:18). Bread figured among their food offerings. Bread also seemed to be their staple diet. Some of Jesus' miracles involved providing bread for the hungry, and it is interesting to note that when he wanted us to grasp the idea of the abundant life he offers us, he refers to himself as 'the bread of life' (Jn 6:35). There is a hunger in the human spirit that no earthly food can satisfy. There is a hole in the human heart that nothing but God can fill. There is an unusual incident in the book of Ezekiel, where the prophet is given a scroll. Ezekiel was being sent on a mission by God to a very wayward stubborn people. Ezekial was told, 'You must give them my messages, whether they listen or not ... Open your mouth and eat what I give you. 'Then I looked and saw a hand reaching out to me, and it held a scroll. The voice said to me 'Son of man, eat what I am giving you – eat this scroll! Then go and give its message to the people of Israel.' So I opened my mouth, and he fed me the scroll. 'Eat it all', he said. And when I ate it, it tasted as sweet as honey' (Ezek 2:7-9; 3:1-3).

I think of this as a very good way to understand how the Spirit of God works in us. Firstly, the message has to be completely consumed, digested, and become flesh within us. Then *we* become the message. 'You write a new page of the gospel each day, by the things that you do, and the words that you say. People read what you write, whether faithful or true. What is the gospel according to you?' You may be the only book some people will ever read, and yet they can come to know Jesus and his

message in and through you. Another story in the Old
Testament points to coming events. Elijah the prophet was given
these instructions by God: 'Go to the east and hide by Kerith
Brook at a place east of where it enters the Jordon river. Drink
from the brook, and eat what the ravens bring you, for I have
commanded them to bring you food.' The ravens brought him
bread each morning (1 Kgs 17:2-4). Later on Elijah came across a
widow with an only son. He asked her for water; as she was
going to get it, he asked her for some bread also. She replied 'I
swear by the Lord your God that I don't have a single piece of
bread in the house. And I have only a handful of flour left in the
jar, and a little cooking oil in the bottom of the jug. I was just
gathering a few sticks to cook this last meal, and then my son
and I will die.' Elijah told her of the Lord's promises, and told
her to go ahead and bake what she had, and the Lord would
look after her. 'So she did as Elijah said, and she and Elijah and
her son continued to eat from her supply of flour and oil for
many days. For no matter how much they used, there was always enough left in the containers, just as the Lord promised
through Elijah' (1 Kgs 17:10-16).

When we reflect on such stories, and then bring ourselves
back to reflect on the Bread that is offered us, surely our hearts
must melt at the wonder of it all. 'Having given us Christ Jesus,
will the Father not surely give us everything else?' (Rom 8:17).
One of the greatest dangers we run is when we begin to take all
this for granted, and it becomes just something we do on Sunday
morning, before returning home for roast, spuds, and mushy
peas for our dinner. I know it's not possible for the human heart
to really grasp the extraordinary and awesome nature of the gift
that is offered. If we could clearly understand the power and
significance of the gift, we would be overcome by our own
weaknesses and inadequacies, in comparison with what is being
offered. It is not necessary that I understand fully. All that is
needed is a genuine *faith/belief* in what I am invited to, and to receive the gift with a real sense of awe, joy, and gratitude. I myself find that Mary, my heavenly mother, is a wonderful help in

all of this. From the time she first held that same body of Jesus at Bethlehem, to the time when she held that same body, now dead, on Calvary, to the many times she received Eucharist, and right up to the time when she embraced her son at the gates of heaven – all of this makes her only too willing to continue her role in me, another of her beloved children. When I was a child, I ran to my mother, absolutely sure that she could fix it, stitch it, bandage it, or make it go away. It's just wonderful that Jesus gives me his own mother to do the same for me today.

Jesus speaks quite a lot of the place of Eucharist on our journey back to the Garden. He multiplied loaves to feed the hungry thousands, and then he went on to speak about another kind of bread that not only feeds the body, and saves lives, but feeds the soul, and gives unending life. 'I assure you, Moses did not give them bread from heaven. My Father did. And now he offers you the true bread from heaven. The true bread of God is the one who comes down from heaven and gives life to the world' (Jn 6:32-33). When the people asked him for that bread every day of their lives, Jesus replied: 'I am the bread of life. No one who comes to me will ever be hungry again' (Jn 6:35). As Jesus continues to become more and more specific and emphatic about his offer, many of his listeners become more and more cynical and incredulous. 'Yes, I am the bread of life! Your ancestors ate manna in the wilderness, but they all died. However, the bread from heaven gives eternal life to everyone who eats it. I am the living bread that came down out of heaven. Anyone who eats this bread will live forever; this bread is my flesh, offered so the world might live' (Jn 6: 48-51). It was at this stage that 'many of his disciples turned away, and walked no more with him', because they considered what he said to be too farfetched and unreal. Jesus didn't run after them to call them back, to give them further explanations, or to water down his message. No, he turned to those who did not walk away, and he asked 'Will you also go away?' (Jn 6:67).

A point needs to be stressed here. Those who walked away made a decision. The reason he challenged the others is that they may not have made any decision, and had just stayed on out of curiosity, fear, or indifference. I honestly have to look at where I stand in all of this. It's so easy to follow the crowd, and just lag along listlessly. The offer from Jesus is infinite, awesome, divine, and enormously and prodigally generous. What a tragedy if it was met with indifference on my part. The world's shortest, and, perhaps, most powerful play, is when Jesus enters heaven at the ascension. The Father says 'I'm sorry, son.' Jesus replies 'Father, it wasn't the nails that hurt as much as the kiss.' Chilling. I cannot see how I could possibly be on the right road, leading back to the Garden, if I do not fully avail of the daily manna that is mine for the taking. Not everybody gets to Mass every day, and that's not what I'm talking about here. I am speaking of the power of Eucharist, as a sustaining, nourishing, and transforming food, available along the way, whenever I can avail of it. It's what happens when I come back out the door after Mass that counts. Where do I go to from here? What difference should it make to my journey today? Mother Teresa (Blessed) says that we in the West have no idea about the pangs of hunger. 'It was a very young girl who taught me one time. I gave her a piece of bread, which she proceeded to eat very slowly, crumb by crumb. "Eat it", I said to her. "Mother, I'm afraid to, because when I eat it, I will be hungry again".' As I come out from Mass I have been nourished with a food which should fill my deepest hungers for all time. I need never experience the *real* hunger of needing to belong, and to be loved.

# Companions on the Way

The Spirit is not given to the individual, but to those who are part of a believing community. When Jesus ascended into heaven, he brought the body he had with him. He sent the Spirit to 'complete his work on earth'. A spirit cannot do anything. An evil spirit needs somebody's hand to plant the bomb, and somebody's tongue to tell the lie. The Spirit of God needs the human voice to speak a word, and the human ears and heart to hear that word. The onus for any power for change does not rest on the speaker or the listener. When both speaker and listener open their hearts, the Spirit empowers the words spoken and heard, and the human heart is enlightened, formed, and transformed.

I am asked to provide my hands for placing on the sick, and any healing that takes place is totally the work of the Spirit. I myself cannot heal, nor am I asked to. I provide the physical element and permit the Spirit to work through that. When I go to pray, I show up, and invite the Spirit to take over. Words, of themselves, say very little. I meet someone who asks me how I am, and my answer can be simply 'OK'. I meet someone else who asks me the same question, and I sit down and tell that person, at some length, just exactly how I am. The different responses result from the spirit in the words of the enquirer. I felt that one person was simply greeting me, while the other really wanted to know how I was. It is the spirit in the words that gives them meaning. I can say a prayer but, if the Holy Spirit is not in my words, I am not praying. I could teach a parrot to say a prayer; but I could never teach a parrot to pray.

When the Spirit came upon Mary, Jesus was formed within her. When the Spirit came upon the apostles, it bound them into a unit, which we call 'church' or, in reality The Body of Christ. I must live and breathe and have my being within the context of being part of a body. 'The bread is one, and so we, though many, form one body, sharing the one bread' (1 Cor 10:17).

I have a responsibility to the community to which I belong, and there is no scope for unattached individualism. Even if I decide to go up to a cave in the mountain, and live as a hermit there – which could be a wonderful thing to do, if that is what God is calling me to do – I still need the approval of the Christian community, before I can be sure that this is of God. A hermit in the Catholic Church is described as 'a man or woman who feely chooses to live in solitude, in order to praise God, and pray for people'. This form of life has re-emerged in recent years and, in recognition of the fact, a special Canon was introduced into the Code of Canon Law in 1983. This states that hermits are recognised by church law as dedicated to God in consecrated life if, at the hands of the diocesan bishop, they publicly profess by a vow the three evangelical counsels (poverty, chastity, and obedience), and then lead their particular form of life under the guidance of the bishop. (My foot cannot go for a walk on its own!)

One of the conditions in forming a body is that all the members be different. If we were all the same, the body would be all heads, or all feet! Just imagine this scenario: I read the gospels for the first time. I am really impressed, and I wonder if this teaching would work in reality. My reflection on the possibility brings me to a point where I am prepared to experiment, to give it a go. I round up a group of people, probably friends or workmates, who agree to be part of the project. I explain the idea of the body, which helps highlight three or four vital issues:

a)    Each one is different, and needs to be different, if we are to form a body.

b)    Each person must be prepared to accept that all of the others are different.

c)    Each one represents a particular gift that is unique to that person.

d)    While each gift is unique to the person, it must be made available to all, if we are to be united as one.

e)   It is only when all the parts are made available that we
     can possibly complete the body.

Just as a human body, though it is made up of many parts, is
a single unit, because all those parts, though many, make one
body, so it is with Christ. In the one Spirit we were all baptised ... and one Spirit was given to us all to drink. Nor is the
body to be identified with any one of its parts. If the foot
were to say 'I am not a hand, and so I do not belong to the
body', would that mean that it stopped being part of the
body? If the ear were to say 'I am not an eye, and so I do not
belong to the body,' would that mean that it is not a part of
the body? If your whole body was just one eye, how would
you hear anything? If it was just one ear, how would it smell
anything? Instead of that, God put all the separate parts into
the body on purpose. If all the parts were the same, how
could it be a body? As it is, the parts are many, but the body
is one. The eye cannot say to the hand 'I do not need you', nor
can the head say to the feet 'I do not need you.' (1 Cor 12:12-
21).

Another way of looking at this is to think of a Christian community in terms of a mirror which I take off a wall, drop on the
ground, and shatter into many pieces. Each potential member of
my Christian community is represented by a piece of that shattered glass. Each person reflects a different perspective of God.
Forming community happens when each person makes available to the group the piece of the mirror that each possesses.
When all the pieces have been put together, then, and only then,
do we reflect the face of God. Let's look at this another way. I
take the engine of a car apart, and I hand a part to each member
of my group. Of course, the parts are different, and some per-
form more important functions than others, but no one part can
propel this car by itself. The building of community is to invite
each person to make available the particular part possessed by
each, so that, together, the car is reassembled and running again.
It is interesting that communism was centred around the same

general idea, with one very central and core difference. There is a world of difference between a system being imposed by a government, and a group of people being inspired by the Holy Spirit to come together, and to form a unity. This is not done by dictat or government proclamation. In the case of the Christian community, it is people who share a common vision, who are enlightened by the same Spirit, and who are called to a common vocation.

My role within the community is best fulfilled through service:

The greatest in the kingdom are those who serve', Jesus told his disciples. 'When Jesus had finished washing their feet, he put on his garment again, went back to the table, and said to them 'Do you understand what I have done to you? You call me Master and Lord, and you are right, for so I am. If I, then, being your Master and Lord, have washed your feet, you also must wash one another's feet. I have just given you an example that, as I have done, you also may do. Truly, I say to you, the servant is not greater than his master, nor is the Master greater than him who sent him. Understand this, and you are blessed if you put it into practice' (Jn 13:12-15).

In the eyes of the world, the great people are those who lord it over others, who possess the power, authority and influence to ensure that others serve them. Mary, our mother, is a wonderful and very real example of extraordinary power, accompanied by humility, faith, and genuine human love. It is unthinkable that she would want to have one over on Elizabeth, Simeon, or Anna, and that she would demand some sort of subservience which she considered her due, because of the privilege that was hers. She was never in any doubt where the source of her many great blessings was. 'He that is mighty has done great things for me, and holy is his name' (Lk 1:49). (Someone said one time that an atheist is someone who is feeling grateful, but has no one to thank.) Mary remained with Jesus on Calvary, while most of his fair-weather friends ran away. As she gathered with the apostles in the Upper Room, to await the coming of the Spirit, it is inconceivable that she would have anything other than very very gentle, understanding, compassionate, and encouraging words for the apostles. She was behaving towards them as they would be expected to behave towards others, once the Spirit came to empower them. All of these inner dispositions of humility, service, and responsibility towards others are directly the result of the working of the Spirit within our hearts. It is not a question of the Spirit forming the body, and then going off, allowing the body to function as it will. Pentecost is but the beginning of a process. When the Spirit came upon Mary, there began within her a process of gestation that resulted in the body of Christ being presented to the world. Through the work of the Spirit, we are now in that process of gestation, until the body of Christ is formed with us. 'Little children, for whom I am in labour until Christ be formed in you' (Gal 4:19).

When I was growing up, I considered it my greatest responsibility to do everything within my power to ensure than I went to heaven when I died. I still consider this a very laudable goal, of course, even if my approach would be entirely different. In the account of the ascension of Jesus, we are told: 'As soon as Jesus said this, he was taken up before their eyes, and a cloud hid him from their sight. While they were still looking up to heaven, two men dressed in white stood beside them, and said "Men of Galilee, why do you stand here looking up at the sky? This Jesus who has been taken from you into heaven, will return in the same way as you have seen him go there".'(Acts 1:9-11). In other words, instead of looking up into heaven, begin to look all around you, because Jesus said that it is there that we will find him now. 'Whatever you do to the least of these, I will take as being done to me' (Mt 25:45). In other words, instead of concentrating on getting to heaven, my Christian vocation asks me to do what I can to get heaven down here. There are people around me living in hell. 'Make me a channel of your peace. Where there is hatred let me sow your love. Where there is despair, let me bring your hope. Where there is hunger, let me bring your food.' It is more difficult to get heaven into people than to get people into heaven.

In today's world, it is difficult to think of a parish as being a community; rather it is a community of communities. The days of belonging to a large homogenous group, all marching to the beat of the one drum, are over. Within every parish there is now emerging many smaller and different entities, e.g. SVP, Legion of Mary, Charismatic Prayer Group, Bible Study Group, Centring Prayer Group, etc., etc. As in the early church, once again people are beginning to gather together in their homes for prayer, for Eucharist, for sharing the Word of God. Not everybody is free to avail of one of these groups but, for those who can, I strongly recommend it. As a matter of fact, I will finish this section with the following thought: If you say to me, 'If I come across a group of people who are radically living the gospels, I will join them', I will be forced to reply, 'No, that is not how it works! When you are ready to radically live the gospel, you will come across such a group and, if there isn't one, you'll set up one. If you're not ready, you will never find the group, even if there's one next door to you.'

Let's keep in mind that the general theme of this book is our journey back to the Garden. This chapter is intended to remind us that I must not venture out on my own. On many occasions I had the privilege of accompanying pilgrimages to different shrines and places of significance in the gospel stories. I was always impressed how a group of people assembled at Dublin airport, each one knowing probably one other person in the group, and the transformation that had taken place among that same group when we returned to that same airport. We had shared time, experiences, and a common journey over the previous week or two. There was a tangible sense of bonding within the group, with talks of reunions, being in touch, exchanging photographs, etc. It was as if they didn't want to go their separate ways again. When we all arrive back in the Garden, there'll be no 'separate ways' anymore.

# Sign-Posts

A sign post doesn't make me go in a particular direction. It simply points in a particular direction, and the decision is mine as to which way I wish to go. A 'Stop' sign won't bend down and stop me as I approach, nor will a 'Yield' sign switch off the engine of my car, as I approach the intersection. Jesus is the greatest and clearest Sign Post of all time, but even he will not compel us to travel in a direction we choose not to. He said he was the Way (Jn 14:6), not one of the ways. He said there is no other way back to the Garden except through him. 'They who follow me will not walk in darkness, but will have the light of life' (Jn 8:12). The gospels provide a very clear map of the journey we are asked to take, and every twist and turn on the road is clearly marked. People who set out to climb Mount Everest, or travel to the South Pole, will give meticulous attention to planning and mapping out every step of the journey. Jesus detailed our maps for us, because he came in person and travelled that road, ahead of us. He cleared the landmines, and he put down very clear markers. 'By this will all people know that you are my disciples, if you have love one for another' (Jn 13:36).

Rules and laws, where just, are there to protect us, to guide us, and to assist us. It would be irresponsible to allow drivers go down the main street of the town at 100 km per hour. Nor would it be tolerable in any way for an individual to decide who should live, and who should die in his neighbourhood. Any rules and guidelines given to us by Jesus are given entirely out of love, and are totally motivated by what is best for us. If he asks us to forgive others, for example, he does so because he knows only too well the self-destruction that goes with resentments, and harbouring grudges. One of the more detailed maps for Christian living is to be found in what we call the Beatitudes. Let me present them here in some sort of simple paraphrased version, just to make sure that it is clearly understood what Jesus said, and what I am writing about (Mt 5:1-12).

- Blessed are those people who are detached from riches, and have the spirit of the poor, for theirs is the kingdom of heaven.
- Blessed are those who love enough to mourn over the death or misfortunes of others, because they shall be comforted.
- Blessed are the meek and the gentle, because everything will come to them.
- Blessed are they who yearn and long for justice for others, because they will be satisfied.
- Blessed are those who are merciful and forgiving towards others because that's what they themselves will receive.
- Blessed are those with a pure heart, who deal honestly and sincerely with others, because they shall see God.
- Blessed are those who work for, and try to promote peace, because they will be called children of God.
- Blessed are those who are made to suffer because of the good they do, because the kingdom of heaven is theirs.
- Blessed are you when people treat you badly because you are my friends, and you are trying to live as I ask you. Be glad and be happy, because your reward will be great in heaven.

These Beatitudes (Be-Attitudes?) give us clear guidelines for our own attitudes, dispositions, and actions. The end of the line, the Garden, is what Jesus calls the kingdom of heaven, or the kingdom of God. The necessary requirements are being gentle, poor in spirit, concerned about others, and purity of heart. If there was a border-crossing on the way, requiring visa or passport checks, these would be the credentials I would have to present, before continuing on the journey. If we all were arrested, brought down to the local police-station, and charged with being Christian, how many of us would get off scot-free for lack of evidence?

The early Christians must have seemed a very strange bunch, indeed. They were followers of someone who was executed as a public criminal, and their whole message was that this man was still alive. There was no sign of him around the place, like there had been a few years previously, but they stubbornly insisted on speaking about him in the present, as someone alive and well, and living among them. There was one thing, however, that did impress them, and they could not deny it. 'See how these Christians love one another' was the comment they made among themselves. There was no denying the evidence of their eyes, which is exactly the kind of witness that Jesus asked of them. They were to be his witnesses, more through how they lived and behaved than anything they preached. Like him, they were to become sign-posts to others, pointing to a Way. Before they became to be known as Christians (a derogatory title given them in Antioch), they were known as followers of the Way. Jesus was the Way, he showed the Way, and he sent his Spirit to guide our feet into that Way. That Way would definitely, without a doubt, lead us back safely to the Garden.

Love, for the Christian, is not some romantic esoteric emotion; some sort of feel-good experience that enables us go around loving everybody! Far from it. This love is about dying, and nothing less than that. 'Greater love than this no one can have, than to be prepared to die for another' (Jn 15:13). Love is about forgiveness, tolerance, patience, humility, understanding, and compassion. It involves unscrewing the top of another's head, looking out through their eyes, and trying to see things as they appear to them. There are very clear markers along the road of Christian love. 'Love your enemies, do good to those who hate you. Bless those who curse you, and pray for those who treat you badly … Do to others as you would have them do to you … Be merciful, just as your Father is merciful. Be not a judge of others, and you will not be judged; do not condemn and you will not be condemned; forgive, and you will be forgiven; give, and it will be given to you, and you will receive in your sack good measure, pressed down, full and running over, for the measure you give will be the measure you receive back'(Lk 6:27-38). My reason for quoting Jesus at some length is, firstly, because what he says is so simple and direct and, secondly, it shows that there are very clear markers all along the road to the Garden. I am told how to act and react in each and every situation. The script is written for me well in advance, but there is something much more important than that: I am given the Holy Spirit, so that I will be able to live out that script as written. 'That we might live no longer for ourselves, but for him, he sent his Holy Spirit as his first gift to those who believe, to complete his work on earth, and to bring us the fullness of grace.' Jesus wrote the script, and the Spirit is the Producer and Director. Each of us has a vital role in this real-life drama. We know how the story ends. That's one great advantage. To know, right from the beginning, that the story ends with resurrection must surely be a wonderful sustainer, when the going gets tough along the way.

When one or two mountaineers decide to take on Mount Everest, there is much preparation to be made. All previous attempts, whether successful or failures, are examined in detail. Advice is sought from those who have attempted this before, so as to benefit from their experience and insights. One of the most important elements in all the preparation, however, is to get a good local guide; to get someone who knows every nook and cranny of the mountain, and every twist and turn of the weather. These are the unsung heroes of all such ventures. Without Tensing, Hillary would never have reached the summit, and he was the first to admit that. On our Christian journey, with all its sign-posts, we are also accompanied all the way, and our guide is the Spirit and Breath of God. It is the Spirit who fills our sails, and moves us along, as we ride the wind.

Migrant birds completely fascinate me. I just cannot comprehend how a tiny little bird can leave the Ivory Coast on a fixed day each year, and land in the slob-lands of Wexford. What is even a greater source of wonder is what happens at the end of the summer. By then the young chicks are moving about and, in early September, the parents fly back to the Ivory Coast and the chicks follow them about a month later, and arrive in the exact same place! I would like trying to explain that to an adult, not to

mention a child. (The child would probably be the least surprised!) I think of such a phenomenon when I reflect on the direction given to our lives by the Spirit. I have no doubt that, if
these birds were given free will, as we are, one of them might decide to fly to New York instead, and end up very dead indeed in
the middle of the Atlantic. Free will is an extraordinary gift, but
it can also pose a frightening threat. To give us free will is God's
way of showing his trust in us; in giving us the responsibility for
making our own decision; in freeing us from the ignominy of
being mere robots, totally incapable of making a decision of our
own. As with all privileges, there follows the responsibility, and
each of us is asked to take responsibility for our own actions. I
said earlier in this chapter that a sign-post points towards a
place, but it won't make me go in that direction. It is the same
with the Spirit. The Spirit leads … into all truth … into the ways
of peace. Jesus offers me peace, but I'm totally free to live in mis-
ery and die of ulcers, if I choose to. The key that opens my heart
to God is willingness. Unless I am prepared to make this key
available, then Jesus has to stand at the door and knock. He will
not come in unless I open the door. Like the Spirit, Jesus is inter-
ested in leading, not in driving or dragging. 'Peace on earth to
those of goodwill' (Lk 2:14).

Jesus came across a man who had spent thirty-eight years sitting by a pool. Once a year the waters of the pool moved in
miraculous fashion, and the first into the water at that time was
healed. This man waited for his chance all those years. When
Jesus came along, he saw the man, and he asked him a simple
question 'Do you want to get healed?' (Jn 5:6). Seems a strange
question, doesn't it? Perhaps, if the man had really wanted to be
healed he would have succeeded by now. Whatever the reason, I
refer to this now because, as I finish this chapter on the sign-
posts to the Garden, Jesus could very well ask me 'Do you want
to get back to the Garden?'

# *Splinters*

'If any of you wants to be a disciple of mine, you must be willing to take up your cross every day, and follow me' (Mt 16:24). 'And whoever does not take up his cross and come after me is not worthy of me. He who cares only for his own life will lose it; he who loses his life for my sake will find it' (Mt 10:38-39). At this stage we enter into one of the most sublime, central, and most misunderstood parts of the Christian message, and the least attractive part of the Christian journey. This is both understandable and sad. Understandable, because suffering of itself is never attractive. Sad, because, when properly understood, it is the most joyful and life-giving element of Christian living.

Our human instinct for self-perpetuation is so strong that it is true to say, in general, nobody likes to die. Some people can be so sick or so old, that they long for the release of death but, under normal circumstances, it is quite natural to want to cling to life as long as possible. I think we must begin by clarifying what exactly we mean by the word and the idea of 'death'. Death is an end of life as we know it. It is the end of a journey, and probably the *end*. And then Jesus comes along, and changes everything … Because of what he has done, death has been transformed utterly, and is not what it was when it entered as weed into the good wheat of our creation. Satan brought death, just as deceits and lies mediate death to those around us. Only the truth can set us, and others, free. When Jesus took on our human nature, he took it on completely. That meant that he had to see it right through, out to the very end. The 'final enemy' was death and, if he had stopped short of that, we would not be free. 'If Jesus has not risen from the dead', says Paul, 'our faith is in vain' (1 Cor 15:17). Jesus would change the whole scenario of death for all time. Death was nailed to the cross with him on Calvary, and lay in utter defeat as he appeared triumphant on Easter morning. The cross is the sign of victory over death.

What does it mean when we are asked to take up our cross and follow him? It does not mean that we, too, will end up on Calvary although, for many of his followers it has meant that they paid for their discipleship with their lives. For the rest of us, though, our cross is not so dramatic, or so obvious. It is seldom a once-off, major news-worthy event, but consists of the splinters of everyday living. It is as if my cross is made up of splinters strewn along the road of life; all those little trials, tests, and temptations that require the generous response of a Christian heart. It involves dying to self for the sake of another, by putting other people's welfare ahead of my own. Selfishness and self-preoccupation is very insidious, cunning, baffling, and very very patient. We have to be continually on our guard against it because, most of the time, we will completely fail to notice it. It is only the Spirit of Truth who can alert us to the reality, and only then can/will we be set free.

> Then the mother of James and John came to Jesus with her sons, and she knelt down to ask a favour. Jesus said to her 'What do you want?' And she answered, 'Here are my two sons. Grant that they may sit, one at your right hand, and the other at your left hand, when you are in your kingdom.' Jesus said to the brothers, 'You do not know what you are asking. Can you drink the cup that I have to drink?' They answered, 'We can'. Jesus replied 'You will indeed drink my cup …' (Mt 20:20-23).

One of the most intriguing parts of the whole economy of salvation is that, while it involves pure free gift, yet we are allowed to play our part, to be involved, and to carry some of the burden, and come into full possession of all of the triumph. 'You know that when we go to Christ through baptism we are all baptised and plunged into his death. By this baptism, this death, we were buried with Christ, and as Christ was raised from among the dead by the Glory of the Father, so we must walk in new life. We have been buried with him to share in his death, in a symbolic way; and so we also share in his resurrection' (Rom 6:3-5). Christ became identified with us when he took on our humanity. We are asked to become fully identified with him in his death and resurrection.

Let's have a look at Calvary for a few minutes. It was there that the final battle with evil was fought and won. Some people stayed, while others ran away. From a human perspective, it represented total and abject failure. That is the extraordinary paradox of suffering. 'It is in dying that we're born to eternal life.' If I had actually been on Calvary on Good Friday, I wouldn't bet on it that I would have remained there with Mary. Of course, if I did stay near enough to her, I would hear what I hear today about the church: 'Stay as you are, where you are, because Easter is only around the corner.' Mary 'heard the word of God, and kept it' (Lk 11:28). 'All these things happened to you, because you believed that the promises of the Lord would be fulfilled' was Elizabeth's greeting to her (Lk 1:45). The extraordinary and wonderful good news about Calvary is that I can actually be there for every moment of every day, if I choose. I am not at all speaking of constant suffering here, as with Saint Pio, and many other chosen souls. Calvary was Jesus saying 'Yes' to the Father, and I can add my 'Yes' to Jesus, to his 'Yes' to the Father, any time of the day I choose. I do this every time I place a drop of water in the chalice at the Offertory of the Mass. The chalice represents the death of Jesus. 'Father, if it's possible, let this chalice pass from me …' (Lk 22:42). The drop of water that I place in the chalice is a symbolic return, one drop at a time, of the waters of my baptism. I am living out my baptism every day, through the many ways I am called upon to die to self, for the sake of others. These are the splinters, because it's only very special souls that have been entrusted with the cross.

In the gospel story we are told that Jesus died on Friday, and rose to new life on Sunday, but that need not be our experience. I have a friend in hospital. I am tired, and the last thing I want to do is to battle city traffic as I cross town to visit him. For his sake

I make the sacrifice. Without exception, I have found in such a situation, that I am already experiencing Easter as I'm coming back out of the ward. Whatever dying it required, it led to immediate new life, for me and, hopefully, for my friend. I think it must be obvious, to those who wish to see, that I cannot really love another without being prepared to take on the dying that it is sure to include. No matter how much a mother loves her newborn baby, she isn't exactly over the moon when the baby cries all night, or pukes all over her just as she was about to put the baby down for the night. OK, there are many ways of dying, and some of them are easier and come more naturally than others. Jesus speaks about loving our enemies, but it's often quite a test to be able to love our friends! The Christian life is no Don Quixote mission.

The kingdom of God is built up in two ways: by tiny acts of goodness, and most of them are hidden and unknown to others. Any one of us can be really involved in the building and promoting of the kingdom if, of course, we are prepared to die quietly in the process. The secret of Pentecost is to be able to die quietly! I'm not asked to be a John Wayne walking down the main street at high noon, ready to show the world just how brave and fearless I am. It's not easy to die but the irony of it is that such people are among the happiest people in the world. Following Jesus can sound very romantic and glamorous, but it is in the everyday, day-in day-out, humdrum experience of living and dying that the bond is forged with him, and we begin to experience new life within, and the presence of the Spirit in all that we do and say. 'The greatest in my kingdom are those who serve' (Lk 22:27). Holiness is not something I do or cause; rather is it something that happens to me. It is like the drip-drip of water on a stone, or the chip-chip of the sculptor's chisel on the marble that begins to transform, to smooth out the edges, and allow a whole new image to emerge. In our case, that image is Jesus Christ. We are like uncut diamonds in the hands of a master craftsman. Only he can see the possibilities. I am absolutely certain that if I could be given a glimpse of what the Spirit sees as he looks at any one of

us, I would be totally gob-smacked. Oh, yes, he would see us as
we are, something that we ourselves could never really hope to
see. But he would see much more than that. He would see what
we can become, if we allow him work in us, through us, and
with us. That is certainly something that far exceeds our most
vivid imaginations. This process of dying, of being reborn, of beginning again each new day, all of this is the journey which, believe it or not, is an end in itself. There was a time in my life
when I thought of this life as something to be endured, while the
real life would begin after we die. In a way, that is true, but not
literally true. The road to heaven is heaven and, for those who
share in Calvary now, is given the wonderful privilege of sharing in Easter now. I do not have to wait till I die to begin to enjoy
eternal life. The life that the Spirit gives us is eternal, and it is
now.

> Six days later, Jesus took with him Peter and James and his
> brother John, and led them apart up a high mountain. Jesus'
> appearance was changed before them; his face shone like the
> sun, and his clothes became bright as light. ... Peter spoke,
> and said to Jesus, 'Master, it is good for us to be here. If you
> wish, I will make three tents: one for you, one for Moses, and
> one for Elijah.' (Mt 17:1-4).

It is easy to understand why Peter felt the way he did. This was
magnificent, it was glorious, it was profoundly impressive.
However, Jesus knew and saw differently. They had to come
down off that mountain, because there was still much more to be
done. There was another mountain (Calvary) that had to be
faced, and what the apostles witnessed on the mount of transfig-
uration was but a glimpse of how things would be after Jesus
had completed his mission. It could easily be tempting to stay on
that mount, but Jesus came with a mission, and 'how can I be at
peace until it is accomplished?' (Lk 12:50). Just before he died on
Calvary we are told 'Jesus took the vinegar, and said "It is accomplished." Then he bowed his head and gave up his spirit' (Jn
19:30). At last, the struggle is over, the victory is won, and it very
soon will be time to proclaim that victory. It is part of our voc-

ation, right down to this day, to continue proclaiming that victory. 'Since we have died with Christ, we will also rise with him' (Rom 6:8).

I want to finish off this chapter by probably stressing the obvious: dying is what a Christian is asked to do during life. Death is like a pile of sand at the end of my life, which I can take a little each day and sprinkle along the road as I travel, so that, when I reach the end, my dying will have already happened, and I will enter straight into the fullness of life. I like to think that, once we arrive at the gates of the Garden, we would be invited to come in right away. 'Father, since you have given them to me, I want them to be with me where I am, and see the Glory you gave me, for you loved me before the foundation of the world. Righteous Father, the world has not known you, but I know you, and these have known that you have sent me. As I revealed your name to them, so will I continue to reveal it, so that the love with which you have loved me may be in them, and I also may be in them' (Jn 17:24-26). 'I'm gonna leave this burden down' will be a song for our return to the Garden. The cross is now replaced by a crown. All along the way we were told again and again that this is how our journey would end, and we trust the Spirit to keep that promise clearly before our minds. I say once again something I have said in an earlier chapter: The only real sin I can commit, as a Christian, is not to have hope.

# Staying On-Line

'The Branch cannot bear fruit by itself but has to remain part of the vine; so neither can you if you do not remain part of me. I am the vine and you are the branches. As long as you remain in me, you bear fruit; but apart from me you can do nothing. Whoever does not remain in me is like a branch that is thrown away and withers; and the withered branches are thrown into the fire and burned' (Jn 15:4-6).

One of the memories I have of childhood was an old woman living in our part of the country who kept goats. Everywhere she went, the goats followed her. It was not unusual to meet her coming along the road with a dozen goats trotting along behind her. What fascinated me about the goats was that they were tied together, as they trotted along freely – but, definitely, all in the one direction. I am aware that this is a very limping example to use when I speak of us travelling back to the Garden with Jesus. Jesus calls himself a shepherd, not a goat-herd. What was un-usual about the old lady, among many other things, is that the goats followed her. You can lead sheep, and they will follow, but you have to drive goats, because they will follow nobody. 'When the Son of Man comes in his glory with all his angels, he will sit on the throne of Glory. All the nations will be brought be-fore him and, as a shepherd separates the sheep from the goats, so will he do with them, placing the sheep on his right, and the goats on his left' (Mt 25:31-33). The sheep represent those who followed Jesus voluntarily, and the goats are those who refused to follow, or who had to be driven along the path of righteous-ness, because of fear of domestic, civil, or divine retribution.

Jesus speaks about 'remaining in me'. In simple, everyday language, what does that mean? Let me use the example of the

computer here in front of me as I write. To send messages to others, or to check on news, weather, or other data on national and
international levels, I have to be connected with a telephone system that will link me up with where I wish to contact. This is
called being 'on-line'. With the progress of modern technology, I
can avail of what is called 'broadband', which is a permanent
connection, which gives me immediate access to the facility for
sending messages or seeking information. When I am connected
to Jesus, I am 'on-line', and this is definitely 'broadband'! For
many years of my life I didn't understand this simple truth. I
was always connecting and disconnecting, when it came to
prayer. Switching from prayer to work was like unplugging one
gadget, and plugging another into the same socket. It was
'change-over' time, when time could be strictly compartmentalised. Notice, it is only my head that changes gear; the heart,
lungs, etc., just continue as usual. When I discover that prayer is
a heart-thing, and not a head-thing, then I continue to have a
praying heart in the midst of the marketplace. I could be in the
midst of the maddening crowd, and still have a hermitage in my
heart. The secret here is to be deeply and constantly aware of the
source of prayer, grace, gift, spirit. This is all the work of God,
and God never has to change gear or switch plugs. As a source
of life, love, and power, the Spirit is always available to me, and
I can draw from that source in every single thing I do. To live
with conscious awareness of this source, and to have a sense of
being connected to it at all times, is what it means to remain in
Jesus, and allow him remain in us.

'I live now, not I, but Christ lives within me' (Gal 2:20). 'You
are not under the control of the flesh, but of the spirit, because
the Spirit of God is within you. If you did not have the Spirit of
Christ, you would not belong to Christ. But Christ is within you'
(Rom 8:9-10). 'Who shall separate us from the love of Christ?
Will it be trials, or anguish, persecution or hunger, lack of clothing or dangers or sword? ... No, in all this we are more than con-
querors, thanks to him who has loved us. I am certain that neither death nor life, neither angels nor spiritual powers, neither

the present nor the future, nor cosmic powers, were they from heaven or from the deep world below, nor any creature whatsoever will separate us from the love of God, which we have in Christ Jesus our Lord' (Rom 8:35-39). I have quoted at some length here, because I could not hope to improve on the powerful conviction of Paul about that umbilical chord that binds us to Christ at all times.

Let me make a point, though, that needs constant stressing. 'Who will separate us from the love of Christ?' Only ourselves can do that. When I speak of separating from the love of Christ, I don't mean that it's possible to stop that love being poured out for us. What I mean is that, of my own accord, I can cut myself off from that love, and refuse to let it reach me. There's a light over the computer here as I write, and it is also lightening up my face, and most of the room as well. I can walk away from here, walk out the side door, and be in total darkness, if I so choose. The light is still shining, of course, and if I return to this desk, it will continue to do for me what it is doing for me now. Jesus didn't want Judas to go out and hang himself, but he couldn't stop him, if that's what Judas decided to do. Once again, it is willingness on my part that makes everything possible. 'Peace on earth to those of goodwill' (Lk 2:14). 'God makes us holy by means of faith in Jesus Christ, and this is applied to all who believe, without distinction of persons' (Rom 3:22). In other words, there are two parts to our salvation: there is what Jesus did, and whether we accept that or not. The work is done, the victory gained, the invitation is offered. The Lord then waits for our response. If we choose to remain connected to him, then we are plugged into the power that will bring us safely all the way back to the Garden.

There are many ways that help us keep connected to Jesus, and my individual preference may be the best one for me. No matter where I place the emphasis in the process, I must always remember that it is the same Spirit working in and through all of us that makes any or all of this possible. Over the years, I have had the privilege of writing some books of gospel reflections, and I found this a very powerful way of becoming immersed in Jesus and his message. It is a continuing on-going experience, of course, and I am never going to get it together, this side of the grave. However, I have to keep going, doing something, and living something for its own sake, and not for the sake of any Brownie points I might earn along the way. Getting to know the mind and heart of Jesus is priceless knowledge in itself. The journey is an end in itself.

There was a certain element of 'Live horse, and you'll get grass' in the religion I inherited. Life was something to be endured. We lived with the fate that befell Adam and Eve, as if Jesus had not come to undo all of that.

> To the woman God said, 'I will increase your suffering in child-bearing, and you will give birth to your children in pain. You will be dependent on your husband, and he will lord it over you.' To the man God said, 'Because you have listened to your wife, and have eaten from the tree of which I forbade you to eat, cursed be the soil because of you! In suffering you will provide food for yourself from it, all the days of your life. It will produce thorn and thistle for you, and you will eat the plants of the field. With sweat on your face you will eat your bread, until you return to clay, since it was from clay that you were taken, for you are dust, and to dust you shall return' (Gen 3:16-19).

Through what he has done, Jesus has changed the whole script for all time. His part of the salvation and redemption story is completed, while ours is always on-going. He is already back at the right hand of the Father, while we are still on pilgrimage. For a number of years I had the privilege of accompanying groups to the Holy Land. A pilgrimage is not exactly intended as a holiday, with every creature-comfort available at the snap of a finger. It was an attempt to walk in the steps of Jesus, and to relive these great moments in the very places where they occurred back then. What amused me (annoyed me?!) was when members of the group made a habit of complaining about the hotel, the coach, the walks – indeed, at some stage or other, the leaders and the Spiritual Director were the subjects of complaints as well. I can well understand that people had paid a lot of money to come on this trip; some were elderly, and many were tired; some were anxious, and some were unwell. It would be unrealistic to expect that everyone should become heroic, and that personalities should change, just because we had moved to a different locale. However, with whatever sensitivity I could muster, I tried to remind people that we were, after all, attempting to walk in the steps of Jesus, and we cannot expect that this will always be easy. In fact, the hardest place to practise the gospel at times is in my own kitchen.

Eucharist is obviously a very real way of maintaining the sense of being in Christ, and Christ being in us. I open my heart as well as my mouth when I receive communion. I welcome him into my heart, and I ask him to make his home there. This is my favourite prayer, which I often share publicly after communion:

Lord Jesus, we welcome you, and thank you for coming. We ask you to make your home, feel at home, and be at home within our hearts. Set up your kingdom there, proclaim your victory, and hoist that flag of your victory within our hearts. Put all enemies there under your feet. Take your whip of cords and drive out anything within our hearts that's not of you. Come with us into this day, Lord. Keep us close to you, and don't let us be apart from you today. May your presence within us touch the hearts of those we meet today, either through the words we say, the prayers we pray, the lives we live, or the very people that we are.

'He humbled himself by being obedient to death, death on the cross. That is why God exalted him, and gave him the Name which is above all names, so that at the name of Jesus every knee should bow, in heaven, on earth, and among the dead, and all tongues proclaim that Jesus Christ is Lord to the glory of God the Father' (Phil 2:8-11). Repeating the name of Jesus is a very simple and a very powerful prayer. It can become like a mantra, that keeps going, completely unknown to anyone, as I go about my daily business. It is not possible to quantify the presence of

Jesus, but if I am in the habit of repeating his name, then I can be assured that I am in him, and he is in me. I am connected; I am on-line. His name is my password, and it allows me full access to the treasures of heaven. I can make a connection between my breathing, and whispering his name. I can associate his name with every breath I take; and, as I exhale, I can breathe out everything within that is not of him. In doing this, I have Jesus constantly in my heart and on my lips. When a little toddler begins to pick up words the first ones taught by proud parents are mammy/daddy. This is the parents' way of strengthening the bond, and of giving the baby further security. The baby may not yet know what the words actually mean, but this is the beginning of a process, and a wonderful point on their journey together.

It is obvious that if I remain in Jesus, and he in me, that I cannot go too far astray. Unlike the old woman's goats, we don't have to be tied together! To walk with Jesus is a personal and deliberate decision. Someone else said yes for me at baptism, and, indeed, my yes of confirmation might not have had the level of maturity required for a life-long relationship. There comes a time in my life, however, when I must take full personal responsibility for my response to my Christian calling. The secret, however, is that this is not simply just a once-off thing, but something that must be renewed with each new day. I can live today on my 'yes' of today. To continue to be on-line today, I had to switch on the computer this morning.

## Land Mines

The road to hell is paved with good intentions while, at times, the road to heaven can be a minefield.

'A great sign appeared in heaven: a woman, dressed in the sun, with the moon under her feet, and a crown of twelve stars on her head. She was pregnant, and cried out in pain, looking to her time of delivery. Then another sign appeared: a huge red dragon with seven heads and ten horns, and wearing seven crowns on its heads … The dragon stood in front of the woman who was about to give birth, so that it might devour the child as soon as it was born. She gave birth to a male child, the one who is to rule all the nations; then her child was seized and taken up to God and to his throne, while the woman fled to the desert where God had prepared a place for her. War broke out in heaven, with Michael and the angels battling with the dragon. The dragon fought back with his angels, but they were defeated and lost their place in heaven. The great dragon, the ancient serpent, known as the devil or Satan, seducer of the whole world, was thrown out. He was hurled down to earth, together with all his angels … When the dragon saw that he had been thrown down to earth, he pursued the woman who had given birth to the male child. Then the woman was given the wings of the great eagle … Then the dragon was furious with the woman, and went off to wage war on the rest of her children, those who keep God's commandments, and bear witness to Jesus' (Rev 12).

I quoted that at some length, because I consider this passage as painting in the backdrop to much of our journey back home to the Garden. No matter what Jesus has done, there is no way that

Satan is going to surrender and admit defeat. Indeed, I can imagine that if Satan were offered forgiveness by God today, he would turn it down, because to accept forgiveness he would have to admit that he was wrong, and he has too much pride to allow that to happen. There is one point in this quote to which I wish to draw attention. I left out parts of it, but if I presented all of Chapter 12, I would read four times that Satan had been cast down to earth. In other words, Satan is not in hell, but is alive and well and living on this planet earth. When Jesus came, he referred to Satan as 'the prince of this world' (Jn 16:11). Satan brought Jesus up to the top of a high mountain (Lk 4:5) and offered him the kingdoms of the world, if he would fall down and adore him. The implication here, of course, is that those kingdoms were Satan's to give.

One glance down the front few pages of my morning newspapers gives evidence that Satan is certainly busy. Why do I say that Satan is not in hell? If hell is a state of total alienation from God, then Satan is certainly in hell. However, the problem is that many people think of hell as a place, and if they believe that Satan is in that place, then he may not be around here too much! 'Be sober and alert, because your enemy the devil prowls about like a roaring lion seeking someone to devour. Stand your ground, firm in your faith, knowing that our brothers and sisters throughout the world are confronting similar persecutions' (1 Pet 5:8-9). 'Give in, then, to God; resist the devil, and he will flee from you' (Jas 4:7).

There are three kingdoms: the kingdom of God, the kingdom of the world, and the kingdom of Satan. The kingdoms of the world and of Satan are happy bed-fellows, because their message is basically similar. The kingdom of Satan is based on lies and deceit, while the kingdom of the world is based on wrong priorities and false values. At the end of time (the world) there will be a very dramatic finale, as the kingdom of this world comes to an end and, yes, Satan is then sent all the way to hell, with all his angels, for ever ever more. No longer will he be able to harm any of God's children who, like the woman in our first quote, will be brought away beyond his range. 'When Jesus reached Gadara on the other side, he was met by two demoniacs who came out from the tombs. They were so fierce that no one dared pass that way. Suddenly, they shouted, 'What do you want with us, you, Son of God? Have you come to torture us before our time?' At some distance there was a large herd of pigs feeding. So the demons begged him, 'If you drive us out, send us into that herd of pigs.' Jesus ordered them 'Go!'. So they left and went into the pigs. The whole herd rushed down the cliff into the lake, and was drowned' (Mt 8:28-32). The interesting thing here is that the demons desperately wanted to be left on this earth, and were terrified that Jesus would send them down before their time had come.

Jesus told us to 'watch and pray, lest we fall into temptation' (Lk 22:40). Notice the order: watch and then pray. It is important for us to be on our guard, because the evil one is extremely cunning, and can tempt us even as we pray. He is also listening to our prayers, and he knows what it is we long for. Therefore, we must constantly, deliberately, and carefully keep ourselves under the protection that is afforded us by the Holy Spirit and by Mary. St John tells us: 'Little children, there is a Spirit in you that is greater than any evil spirit you will meet on the road of life' (1 Jn 4:4). Mary, the woman on whom Satan declared war, has been entrusted with the special task of protecting her children, and of crushing the head of Satan (Gen 3:15). 'You have the anointing of the Holy One, so that all of you have true wisdom. I write to you, not because you lack knowledge of the truth, but because you already know it, and lies have nothing in common with the truth. Who is the liar? He who denies that Jesus is the Christ. He is the antichrist, he who denies both the Father and the Son ... I write to you thinking of those who try to lead you astray. You received from him an anointing, and it remains in you, so you do not need someone to teach you. His anointing teaches you all things, it speaks the truth, and does not lie to you; so remain in him, and keep what he has taught you' (1 Jn 2:20-27).

I mentioned at the beginning of this chapter about the road to heaven being littered with land mines. What I am saying now is that we are supplied with every possible kind of mine detector, and we are asked to avail of these as we go along, and there is no reason why any harm should come to us. Good will always be tested by evil. Human life is warfare, in that there will always be a struggle between what I *want* to do, and what I *ought* to do; between what I *want* and what I *need*; between how I *am*, and how I *ought to be*. It has been suggested by one writer that there could possibly be a meeting at the moment of my death, between the me that I then will be, and the me that God created me to be. Don't worry! God loves you exactly as you are and, so, he will love the you that you are at that time. (When I say that God loves me exactly as I am, I always stick on a little 'rider' to that, but he loves me even more than that, or he'd leave me exactly as I am.)

'The Spirit tells us clearly that in the last days some will defect from the faith, and follow deceitful spirits and devilish doctrines, led by lying hypocrites, whose conscience has been branded by the stamp of infamy' (1 Tim 4:1-2). 'Be quite sure that there will be difficult times in the last days. People will become selfish, lovers of money, boastful, conceited, gossips, disobedient to their parents, ungrateful, unholy. They will be unable to love and to forgive; they will be slanderers, without self-control, cruel, enemies of good, traitors, shameless, full of pride, more in love with pleasure than with God. They will keep the appearance of piety, while rejecting its demands. Keep away from such people' (2 Tim 3:1-5).

I must admit, thankfully, that I'm not one of those who see today's world as a den of iniquity, and who long for a return to 'the good old days', when everything was perfect. May the good Lord continue to protect me from such arrogance! Over the years I have had great admiration for my brothers and sisters who grew to the point of being able to accept that their children were not exact clones of themselves. While being every bit as good as their parents, they have their own ways of doing and seeing things. For my generation, who had a monopoly on right,

on morality, and on proper behaviour, it certainly took some ad-
justing to be willing to 'live, and let live'. OK, a sin is a sin, and if
I see something that I genuinely consider as wrong, I should
have the moral courage to say so, if life has placed me in a position where I have a right to comment. I know I am getting side-
tracked in this paragraph, but I went down this line just to point
out that each generation presents a new challenge to Christian
living. Quite recently, we had the EU (European Union) failing
to include any mention of God in its Constitution. The world is
becoming more secular, and the spiritual is becoming more marginalised. I honestly confess that this does not worry me, because I just have to believe that the Spirit is quite capable to
working through each and every object thrown in the path of the
Christian message, and the living of that message. Rather than
think of the problems facing the Christian in today's world, I
think it would be more important to see these as opportunities
or challenges.

In life, the miles stretch ahead of us, but the things that mess
up our lives are inside us. 'What comes out of a person is what
makes him unclean, for evil designs come out of the heart: theft,
murder, adultery, jealousy, greed, maliciousness, deceit, inde-
cency, slander, pride, and folly. All these things come from
within, and make a person unclean' (Mk 7:20-23). What I'm saying here is that many of the land mines can come from within.
There is some sort of basic rebelliousness within the human spirit,
and it is the ongoing work of the Spirit to tame that, and bring it
all under subjection to the reign of Christ. When scripture
speaks of us being surrounded by evil on every side, we must
also remember that this evil can be within us as well. We are
earthen vessels – extremely frail, and fragile. We need to place
ourselves constantly under the protection of the Spirit. It may
sound a contradiction, but we really have no reason to be afraid,
if our confidence is properly placed. If we trust in ourselves, we
are doomed to death and destruction. If we trust in the Spirit,
and in the promises of Jesus Christ, then our victory is assured.
The more aware we are of our own weakness, and the dangers

that surround us on every side, the more we will be thrown into the arms of the Lord, and our heavenly mother, and the more our safety is guaranteed. I would go so far as to say that, even if there were no land mines on the road back to the Garden, we could never make it on our own anyhow.

The call to repentance is a wake-up call. 'Arise from your slumber, awake from your sleep.' A new day is dawning! Every new day brings its own tests and trials, as well as its own unique graces and heavenly surprises. To be fully human is to be fully alive. There is a vast difference between living and existing. Everybody dies, but not everybody lives. Part of the attitude of the Christian is to be as fully aware as possible in the living of each day. Each moment can be a moment of grace, if I am alert to the opportunity. I believe it would be really worthwhile to concentrate on the opportunities for good, and the moments of graces, than to become paranoid about the land mines. If I emphasise the positive, I believe I will be protected from the negative. Christianity is really more about what I am for, than anything I may be against.

# Letting Go

The story is told of a man who, when asked for directions to Dublin, replied, 'Well, now, to tell you the truth, if I was going to Dublin, I wouldn't start from here at all.' It is obvious, of course, that if I am to go anywhere, I must begin exactly where I am now. To go to another place is to let go of the place I now occupy. Life involves constantly letting go. This includes age, living conditions, ability to function, control of situations, health, and, eventually, of course, life itself. 'For we have not here a lasting city, but are looking for the one to come' (Heb 13:14). We will never get anywhere if we're not prepared to move. Even if I travel by plane, I have to go to the airport. If I am in a wheelchair, I am still travelling, even if I am physically immobile relative to use of limbs. Time and tide stand still for no one. The minutes, the hours, and the days tick away, and nothing remains the same. To live is to change, and to change is to let go of the present in some way or other. The cycle of the seasons rolls on inexorably, as the leaves falls off the trees, to be replaced by new leaves some months later. The trees cannot hold on to the leaves, nor can they prevent their new adornment of spring attire arriving on cue. 'There is a given time for everything, and a time for every happening under heaven. A time for giving birth, a time for dying; a time for planting, a time for uprooting. A time for killing, a time for healing; a time for knocking down, a time for building up. A time for tears, a time for laughter; a time for mourning, a time for dancing ... Finally, I considered the task God gave to people. He made everything fitting in its time, but he also set eternity in their hearts, although people are not able to embrace the work of God from the beginning to the end' (Ecc 3:1-11).

What goes round comes round and life, once it begins, never ends. The first stage is the womb-life. This is followed a wrenching, a letting go, and emergence into the second stage, through the process of birth. Some mothers suffer varying degrees of post-natal depression, as if the system is hurting because of the pain of letting go of something that essentially has been part of them. The second stage in like being in the womb of God, where we are being formed in the image of Jesus Christ. Once again, this leads to another wrenching, a letting go, and an entry into the third and final stage, through the process that we call death. For those left behind, this is experienced as bereavement, which comes from having to let go of someone who has been part of them. Bereavement is like an amputation. There is part of me gone. I will walk again, of course, but it's only time that can heal this pain. It's only when we all arrive in the Garden that we won't have to say goodbye again. 'On this mountain Yahweh will prepare a feast for all his people, a feast of rich food and fine wines, meat full of marrow, fine wine strained. On this mountain he will destroy the covering cast over all peoples, this very shroud spread over all nations, and swallow up death in victory. The Lord will wipe away the tears from all cheeks and eyes'(Is 25:6-8).

Learning to become detached is a really worthwhile exercise, if understood properly. It is far removed from becoming indifferent or callous. It is a discernment process, and it enables me distinguish between what should be let go, and what should be carefully treasured. There are things I cling to that cause me to be totally encumbered by baggage. I can develop a great need for affirmation, approval and praise, and this can become an obsession which, if not met, creates all sorts of problems within my mind. I cling to daydreams that have no hope of ever becoming realities, where I build castles in the sky that will never be inhabited. I can crave the limelight, and fawn to the powerful. My ego is capable of building up a list of priorities that are mere perceptions of unbridled pride, and built on the moving sands of unreality. It is a very healthy undertaking to look seriously at all

these possibilities, with a view to ascertaining where any or
many might exist. It is a wonderful freedom to be free of such
fantasies. And any letting go involved will repay one hundred
fold. Selfishness and self-centredness is extremely subtle, cunning and powerful, and one of its most insidious qualities is that
it blinds me to its very existence. It is only those who do work on
themselves, or who avail of guidance from others, who become
aware of such lurking dangers. Exposing such dangerous and
destructive impostors is uniquely the work of the Spirit. It is the
work of the Spirit to open my inner eyes and to let me see. This is
the worst form of blindness and no human effort can remove it,
even if it can assist in helping making the situation a bit better. A
genuine desire on my part to really see what exactly those things
are that I need to let go of, nothing short of that will lead to freedom. The discovery is likely to amaze me, because many of the
things I cling to seem quite harmless and innocent in themselves. Put together, though, they can combine to limit my freedom, and to influence my actions and my attitudes. It may seem
totally unreal, but what a gift it must be to be free of all the un-
necessary things that I cling to. I know, in practice, that this
won't happen this side of the grave, but it would be good to
have made a decent and honest start before that time comes
when, without any thanks to me, I'm going to have to let go of
everything anyhow. One of the more obvious ones that jumps
out at me is the whole area of one's self-importance. Humility is
a beautiful gift, and it becomes more realistic when I think of it
as being just another word for truth. Not to be humble, is to be
living a lie. It is to present myself as someone or something that
I'm not. The tragedy about this is that I even come to believe my
own lies in this area. I don't honestly think that I can develop
humility, as I might grow a flower in a garden. If I myself do it, I
could end up being really proud of my humility! 'The meek will
find joy, and the poor among men will rejoice in the Holy One of
Israel' (Is 28:19). It would be a wonderful and very beneficial
prayer to the Spirit to pray day in day out for the gift of insight
into what I should let go of, and what it is that weighs me down,

and holds me back. Pride can be such a tyrant that it is impossible to satisfy its insatiable appetite. There is no way that any progress in this area can come about naturally. A heightened awareness of God's goodness should surely help to shrink the arrogance of my own self-importance. This is a dream to be yearned for, a vision that longs for fulfilment. I owe it to myself to unburden myself of all the myths, unrealities, daydreams, and selfish demands with which my ego can burden me.

'Am gonna leave this old burden down, down by the riverside.' I can imagine Adam and Eve being heavily burdened as they walked away from the Garden. It is because of this that I like to think of the return journey being one that continues to become less and less burdened as life goes on. Our priorities change with the years. Those things that were so central to our lives in young ambition's vision, are not seen to be that central anymore. The focus of life can shift according to circumstances. There is an evolutionary force at work, and we are changing, whether consciously or not. That change is not necessarily for the good. I don't change for the good (or for the bad!) just by accident. OK, so I can 'drift' into the bad, without being fully alert to the ramifications of what is happening, and to the dangers that lie ahead, as I approach Niagara. I cannot, however, drift into good. This involves a series of decisions, a day in, day out acceptance of the presence of the Spirit, and a declared willingness on my part to be open to the work of that Spirit. Of necessity, this has to be a process of letting go. Any change implies letting go, and living is about the whole process of change.

The unborn baby is constantly evolving, and the mother is becoming more and more aware of the growth of life within her. The difference here, of course, is that the baby is not contributing anything to the process. After birth, the baby will get hair, teeth, etc. but, once again, will contribute nothing to speeding up or delaying this process. At our stage in life, however, the lever is in our hand; it is we who press the button. The Spirit is always on standby, but cannot work in us without our permission, freely given. Jesus makes a very important point when he talks about the problem a camel would have, trying to enter by the side gate of the temple. 'Then Jesus said to his disciples, "Truly I say to you: it will be hard for one who is rich to enter the kingdom of heaven. Yes, believe me: it is easier for a camel to pass through the eye of a needle than for the one who is rich to enter the kingdom of heaven".' (Mt 19:23-24). There is a simple lesson here, and it is important to understand it correctly. The side gates to the Temple were called 'needles'. Now a camel could pass through one of these, but only after all the load is removed from its back. It is only after it has shed all of its burden that it can enter those gates. There is nothing wrong with riches, and Jesus is not saying that there is. What he refers to here is the danger of clinging to riches, in the belief that this could even buy me heaven, or guarantee my continued happiness. 'What did he leave?' a local man asked, after a wealthy neighbour died. 'He left nothing. He was dragged away from it!' was the wry reply of his neighbour.

Let's leave the money aside for now, because I am more concerned about the other things we cling to, which are not as destructive, but not so obvious. Over the last decade or so we have witnessed absolutely ferocious and vicious destruction of human lives, of tribes, of a nation's people. Somewhere, in some one's heart, there was an opinion that was not going to be surrendered and, because of this failure to let go, several million lost their lives. There would never be a war if someone somewhere was prepared to say 'I'm sorry; I was wrong.' It sounds awfully simple, and it is, if the Spirit of God is given the slightest chance of entering into the situation. I have no intention of sitting here passing judgement on world or tribal leaders. Such condemnation should be forthcoming, but it's not going to change anything. For any good to come out of this, it must begin within my own heart. I wouldn't shoot a person, or torture them to death. However, I can have more subtle and underhand ways of hurting people. I can cut with a word just as with a sword. I have to be constantly on my guard against that subtle pride which can so easily blind me to the things I cling to at the ex-

pense of others. Is my opinion really that important, after all?
Pride, selfishness, self-centredness, and self-preoccupation can
be such a part of who and what I am that it is impossible to
separate, to isolate, and to look at them objectively. Once again, I
say that this is the work of the Spirit. Again and again, I can de-
clare my willingness to let go, and trust the Spirit to build on my
goodwill. Even my choice of the things that I need to let go can
be very selective, if I keep control of things myself. The Spirit
may notice a trait that is more damaging than is obvious to me. I
have no reason to trust myself in this process, and I have no
need to trust myself either. Surrender, hand over, let go. All of
this implies that Someone else is going to take over, and take it
from here.

The final letting go, of course, is death. If I live with the
process of letting go during my lifetime, I honestly believe that
the sting will be removed from death, and it will be a gentle,
peaceful birth into the fullness of life, where the stream has, at
last, reached the ocean, and just slips in to become part of something infinitely greater. This letting go is symbolised by unclenching the fists, which cling to that last clammy coin; ungritting the teeth, and swallowing our pride; unflexing the muscles,
and allowing the body resume its natural and comfortable position. This letting go involves dropping the masks and revealing
the real me, to discover that both myself and others actually like
what they see. It means that I stop playing games, and begin to
live life with integrity and uprightness. It means coming out
from behind the barriers of insincerity and pretence, removing
the grease-paint of the performer, and walking humbly with my
God. When I am prepared to put my hand in Jesus' hand, and
walk with him, all the way back to the Garden, then I had better
let go of anything my hand clings to. When I let go, I let God,
and nothing is ever the same again.

# The Way Less Travelled

I cannot begin this chapter without acknowledging the source of my title. Some years ago, Scott Peck gave us the classic *The Road Less Travelled*. It made a great impact and, through many types of workshops and workbooks based on that original book, it continues to teach and to inspire. I stopped short of using his title, out of respect, but I could not resist getting as near as I could to it, because it says exactly what I want to write about in this chapter. 'Enter through the narrow gate; for wide is the gate and broad is the road that leads to destruction, and many go that way. How narrow is the gate that leads to life, and how rough the road; few there are who find it' (Mt 7:13-14).

When Jesus had completed his work on earth, he returned in triumph to the Father. Before doing so, however, he gave his apostles their final instructions. 'Go out to the whole world and proclaim the good news to all creation. He who believes and is baptised will be saved; he who refuses to believe is condemned. Signs like these will accompany those who have believed: in my name they will cast out demons, and speak new languages; they will pick up snakes and, if they drink anything poisonous, they will not be hurt. They will lay their hands on the sick, and the sick will be healed' (Mk 16:15-18). Two thousand years later, that mission has had but a minimal effect for good on the world in general, and an enormous effect for wonderful good in the lives of many millions. The mission entrusted to us as Christians has suffered greatly down the centuries. It has suffered greatly in the many and various ways in which it has been interpreted, changed, adopted, and compromised. It has suffered through the perceptions that unfaithful proclaiming and imposing have provided. Where it has been faithfully adhered to, it has suffered at the hands of those who, like the religious leaders with Jesus, knew of only one way to put an end to it, and that is to shoot the messenger. Without the faith that the Spirit inspires, one could easily despair of this message ever getting a wide audience, or attracting widespread attention. If the kingdom of God is not of this world, then neither is the message of God. The Christian message is such a direct contradiction to the beliefs and values of this world, that it would be totally unrealistic to expect it to be acceptable to those whose minds and hearts are moulded and formed by this world. When I think of the message, I must not think of a collection of words strung together, containing great wisdom and sound direction. I must think of the *Spirit* in the words, because words, of themselves, would be incapable of bringing change. On the morning of Pentecost, Peter spoke to several thousands from every land in the known world of the time. His words were so charged with the Spirit that all his listeners heard him speak in their native language, and their hearts were so touched by the power of his words that 'those who accepted his word were baptised; some three thousand were added to their numbers that day' (Acts 2:41). Imagine what would have happened if that momentum had been maintained!

How come that, after all these years, only a minority have ever heard of the Garden, and only a tiny minority of those show any great interest in getting back there? This is something that I cannot pretend to know but I can, at least, express a few opinions on it. Fr Christian de Cherge was the prior in a Cistercian monastery in Algeria, when on 21 May1996, he and six of his confrères had their throats slit by a gang of Muslim rebels. In anticipation of such an event, because of the unleashed violence of Algerian Muslims against all foreigners (the monks were French), Fr Christian had written a letter to Paris, expressing his views, loudly proclaiming his forgiveness to those who might kill them, and asking the French not to blame all Algerians and all Muslims for the actions of a group of extremists. He expresses his admiration for the Muslim religion, in which he finds 'so often the true strand of the gospel'. He looks towards death with 'an avid curiosity' to be able to see things from God's point of view, 'and to contemplate with him his children of Islam just as he sees them, all shining with the glory of Christ, the fruit of his passion, and filled with the gift of the Spirit, whose secret joy will always be to establish communion, and to refashion the likeness, playfully delighting in the difference ...' Here was someone who knew that God has no grandchildren; that we all are children of God. What I mean by this is that I don't believe the Christian message is for everyone, because that would imply that only Christians can make it back to the Garden. In God's way of doing things, such a possibility is unthinkable. I don't pretend, as I've said already, that I fully understand the economy of God's salvation, but I do believe that God is concerned with unity, and never uniformity. Even among the Christian churches, while the emphasis is on uniformity there is no possibility of them ever coming together. It is a question of unity in diversity, that is based on mutual respect. It is not a question of watering down one's beliefs, or compromising one's truth, just to afford accommodation with another church. Ecumenism that is based on dishonesty cannot possibly be of God, and cannot possibly lead to the good. Part of what it means to be a Christian is to have total respect for other religions that are genuinely inspired, are obviously of God, and whose members are sincere fellow-travellers on our journey back to the Garden.

I wrote that last paragraph to 'situate', as it were, the 'other' religions, so that we could get back to our own and see what we ought to do to inherit eternal life (Mt 19:16). No matter which way we look at it, we find ourselves in a minority. Better be in a minority than simply following the crowd, not sure where we are being led. Jesus is very clear about what our presence on this earth should mean. We are like yeast that is mixed with flour in baking a cake; although a tiny portion, it completely effects the whole cake. 'The kingdom of heaven is like the yeast which a woman took, and buried in three measures of flour until the whole mass of dough began to rise' (Mt 13:33). 'Do you not know that a little yeast makes the whole mass of dough rise?' (1 Cor 5:6). We are also compared to salt which gives taste to food, and is a preservative against food going rotten. 'You are the salt of the earth. But if salt lose its taste, how can it be made salty again? It has become useless. It can only be thrown away, and people will trample on it' (Mt 5:13). Isn't it true that only a little salt is needed, and that too much salt would destroy everything? When salt is thrown generously on a road during times of frost, the motorist is advised to run a hose over his car later on, to prevent the damage that so much salt can have even on metal.

We are also referred to as light, and this image is easier to understand. One lit candle effects the darkness in a whole room. Better light a candle than curse the darkness. 'You are the light of the world. A city built on a hill cannot be hidden. No one lights a lamp and covers it; instead he puts it on a lampstand, where it gives light to everyone in the house. In the same way, your light must shine before others, so that they may see your good works, and glorify your Father who is in heaven' (Mt 5:14-16). 'Do everything without grumbling, so that, without fault or blame, you will be children of God without reproach among a crooked and perverse generation. You are a light among them, like stars in the universe, holding to the Word of life' (Phil 2:14-15). All of the above speaks very clearly of the witness factor or value inherent in Christian living. Mother (Blessed) Teresa's witness had a profound effect on the lives of many who are not, or never will be members of the Catholic Church. Christianity is about attracting, not about promoting. 'You will receive power when the Holy Spirit comes upon you; and you will be my witnesses in Jerusalem, throughout Judea and Samaria, even to the ends of the earth' (Acts 1:8). As we all head back to the Garden, then, we discover that different people are marching to the beat of different drums. We share a common destiny. I would much prefer to be a sincere Hindu than a hypocritical or lukewarm Christian. My vocation is to respond with a generous heart to the call I hear; a call that I know is addressed to me.

There are three groups of people in most gatherings, whether that be church, society, or organisation. There are those who cause things to happen; those who watch things happening; and those who haven't a clue what's happening. It is against this that I chose the title about the way less travelled. When I read the description given of the General Judgement (Mt 25), I may be surprised to find that Jesus' questions are scandalously materialistic. He never mentions prayer, attending church, or visiting holy shrines. He speaks about a slice of bread, a cup of water, an item of clothing, a simple visit to a prison. In other words, what I am asked to do is very clearly specified and spelt out, and there is absolutely no room for ambiguity or doubt. Jesus even goes further, lest there be any misunderstanding. He tells us, 'Whatever you do to the least of my brothers and sisters, I will take as being done for me' (Mt 25:40). He really does identify himself very closely with each and all of us; while unashamedly showing a great preference for the poor and the marginalised, just as he did when he walked the roads of Galilee. I can approach Christianity on two different levels. I can approach it as a road-map for life, full of great wisdom, and imbued with wonderful insights. There is enough material and content there to supply the needs of all the world's debating societies, and theoreticians. However, I don't think – as a matter of fact, I'm certain – that this won't change anything. One of the ways of avoiding doing anything is to talk about it long enough.

The second way of looking at Christianity is to be willing to mediate it down to the very specific. In other words, it tells me exactly how I should threat this person in this particular situation. The debating societies may have the advantage of numbers; that is why I speak of our call as walking in the way less travelled. I saw a poster one time which had two doors at the end of a corridor. One door was marked 'Heaven', and there was one person waiting to enter. The other door had quite a crowd waiting to enter, and it was marked 'Talks about Heaven'.

Discovering this Way is one of the Spirit's greatest gifts. 'The kingdom of heaven is like a treasure hidden in a field. The man

who finds it, buries it again; and so happy is he that he goes and
sells everything he has, so that he may buy that field. Again, the
kingdom of heaven is like a trader looking for fine pearls. Once
he has found a pearl of exceptional quality, he goes away, sells
everything he has, and buys it' (Mt 13:44-45). There is something
here that should cause each and every one of us to consider at
some length. If this Way is so important, does our approach to it
show that we do have that conviction? Oh, I know that I can
never be totally committed to anything, in that any level of commitment is capable of being improved on. However, I can get a
fairly accurate reflection of where I'm at relative to travelling
down this road with Jesus. The whole secret, of course, is to
allow myself be led by the Spirit. By myself, I have no way of
measuring or assessing my progress on this journey; nor do I
need to know.

Suffice it to know that my heart continues to be open to the
promptings of the Spirit, and that I take each new day as a gift,
with infinite possibilities. 'For I will gather you from all the nations and bring you back to your own land. Then I shall pour
clean water over you, and you shall be made clean. I shall give
you a new heart, and put a new spirit within you. I shall remove
your heart of stone, and give you a heart of flesh. I shall put my
spirit within you, and move you to follow my decrees and my
laws. You shall live in the land I gave your forefathers; you shall
be my people, and I will be your God' (Ezek 36:24-28). 'There
will be a highway, which will be called the Holy Highway. No
one unclean shall pass over it, nor any wicked fool stray there.
No lion will be found there, nor any beast of prey. Only the redeemed will walk there. For the ransomed of the Lord will return; with everlasting joy upon their heads, they will come to
Zion singing, gladness and joy marching with them, while sorrow and sighing flee away' (Is 35:8-10).

# Pit Stops

'No athlete is crowned unless he competes according to the rules' (2 Tim 2-5). 'I have fought the good fight, I have finished the race, I have kept the faith' (2 Tim 4:7). Pit stops have more to do with car rallies than with marathons, even though the long-distance runner will require a little attention along the way – a bottle of water, a face cloth, or new shoe laces. I am not into motor rallying too much and, so I often find the pit stops to be the most interesting. When I first saw this happening, I thought that it was almost the equivalent of dropping out, until I came to realise that every driver must have a few pit stops, to replace something there, to adjust something here, or simply to top up with gas or oil. It would be tempting not to stop, but this would be very foolhardy in the long run, because the car would become undrivable, and those who had stopped along the way would go swishing by while our friend limps over to the side of the course to let them through. If time spent in the pit stop is time 'wasted' as far as racing is concerned, it is time well-invested in the long-run, and is a necessary and essential part of the race.

As we run the race to which St Paul refers, it is essential that we have pit stops along the way. I refer to much more than prayer here. I don't have to stop to pray! I can continue whatever I may be doing, and still have a heart that is in Prayer Mode. On the other hand, I can stop everything, go aside, and give some quality time to prayer, reflection, and meditation. If I am too busy to do this, then I'm far too busy. I can even become so pre-occupied with the work of the Lord that I haven't time for the Lord of the work. Each one of us is different. Some people are naturally contemplative, and they find it quite natural to take time out, just to sit with the Lord, check in, and listen. They are excellent 'attention-givers' when it comes to prayer. There are others – and I would have included myself among these for most of my life! – who are so busy about many things that they find it really difficult to take time out, and to be still long enough to hear anything. 'Be still, and know that I am God' (Ps 46:10). This quality of being able to walk away from other activities, and give my full attention to God is directly concerned with justice and right living, where I 'render to Caesar the things that are Caesar's, and to God the things that are God's' (Mk 12:17). It avoids the trap of turning the divine initiative into human endeavour. Prayer is really what God does when I give him time and space. It is the time when my soul gets nourished, and enables me walk with greater strength in the ways of the Lord. If I do not have a contemplative spirit, then I have to depend on the Spirit to cultivate this within me. In other words, it is not something that I myself can develop.

The apostles saw Jesus work signs and wonders. They saw him raise the dead, calm the storm, heal the leper, restore sight to the blind. Yet, when push came to pull, what did they ask him? 'Master, teach us to pray' (Lk 11:1). Whatever it was about the way Jesus prayed, this was one thing that they would love to be able to do. Perhaps he was so obviously wrapped up with the Father at such times that those around him felt that this was a moment of great power, and something very special indeed. Jesus himself often went off on his own, for long periods; sometimes all night, at other times very early in the morning, so that he could be alone with the Father. 'And having sent the crowd away, he went up the mountain by himself to pray. At nightfall he was there alone' (Mt 14:23). 'But the news about Jesus spread all the more, and large crowds came to him to listen, and be healed of their sicknesses. As for him, he would often withdraw to solitary places to pray' (Lk 5:15-16). What strikes me about such references – and there are several of them – is that the busier Jesus was, the more time he took out to pray. There is a core lesson in this for all of us, especially those of us who convince ourselves that we are far too busy to have the luxury of making such pit stops. Even taking the time out is a statement in itself. Obviously, I just cannot walk away from work whenever I feel like praying. There are questions about responsibility, justice, and common sense involved here. When I talk about dropping everything, and going aside, I refer to those times when I do have an option, I can make a choice, and the initiative is entirely mine. I'm sure, if we're honest, we can all identify such opportunities.

From what I said earlier, the pit stop is an essential part of the motor rally, and those who decide not to avail of it will never complete the race. I am not speaking of faults or breakdowns, which require immediate attention. Such cars certainly have no chance, if they do not stop; and probably little chance, even if they do. It is simply a fact of life that the car- – the very best – has limitations, and the course is of such a length that tyres will take a ferocious toll, and will need replacement, and the tank cannot hold sufficient fuel for such a distance, if the car is not to be overladen, and lose its accelerating power. Using the example of the pit stop to illustrate the need to come off the roundabouts from time to time, to give time to prayer, is one that begins to limp as we examine it further.

The pit stop is an extraordinary feat of team work, speed, coordination, and return to action. Prayer is certainly not that. I actually believe that if I do begin to take time out to pray, and I am open to the workings of the Spirit in this, those times will become more frequent, and much longer, as time goes on. In other words, I am heading in the opposite direction to the mechanics in the pit stops. The important thing is that I begin. It doesn't matter how short my first attempts are; the important thing is that I have begun what, hopefully, will become a process, and I have no idea where it might lead.

For those who are prepared to take the Christian life seriously, there is no end to the facilities available for building up, and consolidating that life. Days of Renewal, weekend retreats, and workshops on prayer are available in almost every region from time to time. There are adult education courses in spirituality available to those who are free to avail of them. More and more mature Christians are beginning to avail of Spiritual Direction. After all, it is highly advisable to go for check-ups to doctors and dentists, and not wait till the harm is done. Preventative medicine is beginning to get the attention it deserves and, where possible, is the better course to follow. It is better to avail of the warning of the lighthouse than to have to be rescued by the lifeboat. I must say that I have been very edified over the past few years, as I have witnessed so many laity taking responsibility for their prayer-life into their own hands, and no longer leaving this in the hands of priest for an hour on a Sunday morning. There is the danger of God being treated like some sort of income-tax man, where I give him an hour on Sunday, and the rest of the week is take-home money.

It is reasonable to expect that those people who are conscious of being led back to the Garden, should have a constant awareness of the significance of this journey, and how much it depends on the work of God's Spirit. In their journey through the desert, on their way back from exile, the Hebrews often complained of the hardships they endured. 'Then they said to Moses, "Were there no tombs in Egypt? Why have you brought us into the desert to die? What have you done by bringing us out of Egypt? Isn't this what we said when we were in Egypt: Let us work for the Egyptians. Far better serve Egypt than to die in the desert".'(Ex 14:11-12). They were a stubborn and stiff-necked people and, despite the daily manna, and water from the rock, despite the clouds protecting from the sun during the day, and fires protecting them from the cold at night, they still found reasons to complain. Whatever about their physical condition, they certainly weren't too spiritually healthy. It cannot be the same with us, however.

Let me put it this way: I am sitting alone with the Lord. I become more and more aware of his presence. I may speak to him, or I may choose to remain quiet and wait. After a while, while Jesus looks deep within my soul, he looks me straight in the eye, and he asks me a very direct question. 'Tell me this now, honestly, without any attempt to cover up, to impress, or to deny: Is there anything in your live *now* that you are not sure I can take care of? Is there anything there that bothers you, that's eating you inside, that is causing you worry? Can you see from that that this is something you are not certain that *we* can take care of, and that includes the Father, Myself, the Spirit, and my mother? Can you think of any reason why this should be so? Do you think that you could do a better job on your own? Are you afraid that my solution may not be the one that you want, even if it is the better one? If you are to travel the Way with me, you will have to begin to trust me more. You will have to be willing to be led by my Spirit. I would love to teach you the secrets of the kingdom, like I taught the apostles. ('The secrets of the kingdom of God have been given to you. But for those outside, everything comes in parables' [Mk 4:11]). It was when I brought the apostles to one side, away from the crowds, that I was able to do this, and that I taught them to pray. If you don't come aside with me, you are limiting all I want to do for you, and in you.'

In earlier chapters, I spoke of travelling in convoy, as it were; being part of a Christian community. Much of my praying will normally be done within the context of that community, when we join in common worship, which can cover all the spectrums, from Eucharist, devotions, adoration, to prayer meetings. When I speak about pit stops in this chapter, however, I am not referring to any of these. I speak of personal prayer; I speak of the decision that is mine, and mine alone. Taking time out to be with the Lord is part of my personal response to my Christian vocation. This time of prayer is not something that I would like to schedule, so far as making plans or setting guidelines. Generally speaking, it is much better to keep this as spontaneous as possible, even when it does include some of the traditional prayers, such as Rosary, Chaplet of Divine Mercy, etc. An important part of this time should be given to listening. I can also use my creative imagination, as I relive particular scenes in the gospels, where I find that I myself am blind, deaf, dumb, or leprous. There is no end to the scope of the creative imagination, when I sit quietly with the Lord. The secret here is to invoke the Spirit, in the expectation that he *will* lead me, something that is the *forte* of the Spirit. Real prayer is what God does when I give him time and space. I am dealing with the God of Surprises, and I can have no idea where prayer might lead. The important thing is to show up. To do this is half the battle. When I present the body, the Spirit will do the rest. Bring the body, and the mind will follow. Consider these precious times as very central to the journey back to the Garden. It is so easy to get distracted by the scenery along the road, and become less aware of what life is all about. 'Watch and pray' is the advice of Jesus. Going to the Lord is like being awake and alert with him in Gethsemane. It can also seem like standing at the foot of the cross on Calvary, especially when I recite the Divine Mercy Chaplet. All things are possible, but nothing happens if I fail to keep that appointment.

# Riding the Wind

'The wind blows where it pleases, and you hear its sound, but you don't know where it comes from or where it is going. It is like that with everyone who is born of the Spirit' (Jn 3:8-9). There are times when I envy the seagulls! I remember watching a seagull one day, and it went down to the end of a mile-long pier, turned around, and came back again – without moving a wing! It was 'riding the wind', and making the wind do the work. I have watched seagulls having a ball in the midst of a gale storm – twirling, twisting, gliding, and just going with the flow. What a freedom that is!

What a wonderful change it would make in our lives if we could adapt that attitude. The Spirit is the Breath of God, the wind beneath our wings. 'Therefore, I say to you: walk according to the Spirit ... Let the Spirit lead you. The fruits of the Spirit are charity, joy, and peace, patience, understanding of others, kindness and fidelity, gentleness and self-control ... If we live by the Spirit let us be led by the Spirit' (Gal 5:16, 22-25). There are times, of course, when the seagull uses its wings, and it must do so to get where it wishes to go. I can identify that as I watch it come to land on the seashore. It's what happens during that, or after that, that I envy. The sheer freedom of being able to let go, and let the wind lift it right up into the sky, and send it sailing off into the distance. To be able to slightly adjust the wings, and reverse all that first procedure. That must be exhilarating.

I think of the seagull when I think of how life could be. I do believe that God can, and is willing to play a much bigger part in our lives than the one we allow him. I often reflect on the ways in which we, knowingly or unknowingly, must set limits to what he can do in, through, and for us. From pure native instinct, the seagull has a very powerful relationship with the wind. There is a trust there, and a confidence that the seagull and the wind can work together. Life must be very dull indeed, for the poor seagull when everything is 'becalmed', and there's not a puff of wind. It is totally thrown back on its own resources, and I suspect it is more than likely to be seen floating around on the water, or snugly perched in a crevice on the cliff-face. The seagull is OK, though, because the winds will blow again, and it soon will be off on more manoeuvres. What bothers me is when I encounter humans who have no other experience beyond battling the winds, and feeling powerless in the eye of the storm. 'Then a storm gathered and the wind began to blow. The waves spilled over into the boat so that it was already filled with water. And Jesus was in the stern, asleep on a cushion. They woke him, and said to him "Master, don't you care if we sink?" As Jesus awoke, he rebuked the wind, and ordered the sea "Quiet down! Be still!" The wind dropped, and there was a great calm. Then Jesus said to them "Why are you so frightened? Do you still have no faith?" (Mk 4:37-40). Some years ago there was a drought in Israel, and the waters of the Sea of Galilee were at an all-time low. I happened to be there at the time, and I remember standing at the sea shore, with nearly fifty or sixty yards of hardened dried-out mud between me and the edge of the water. Some time prior to my arrival, a discovery had been made in that mud. It was a boat, sticking up ever so slightly. Experts worked very gently, and ever so slowly, and they succeeded in extracting the boat from the mud. It is reckoned to date back to the time of Christ. It is extremely frail and fragile, as was obvious when I went to see it. Its present home is resting on the bottom of a small swimming pool, which is filled with some special kind of preservative liquid. It will probably remain there, because out of that setting it might warp, or disintegrate in some other way. There's no way it could take handling of any kind. Anyhow, to get to the point I want to make! As I looked at that boat, I thought of the incident in the gospel to which I have just referred, and I was in awe. Thirteen men in a boat that size, half-filled with water, being tossed around like a cork on the water, and Jesus is asking them why they were afraid! Not to be terrified in such circumstances would require the highest level of faith I could possibly imagine. And yet Jesus insisted on them learning something from this. I can only dream of what life could be like if I had faith like that.

I remember watching swans on the canal some years ago. I walked past there twice a day on my way to and from work. I was mesmerised by the fact that the swans glided gracefully along, with just the merest ripple of water in their trail. They were majestic. What I could easily overlook, however, is that they were peddaling away underneath! They were working away without making a splash. Lucky swans! They were quite busy, but exuded an aura of calm that was really impressive. Again, what a beautiful image of how life could be.

I know that some people are worriers by nature, and know no other way of being. They are always waiting on the other shoe to drop, and the light at the end of the tunnel must surely be the lights of an on-coming train! This can easily become a way of life and, as with the man at the pool, Jesus could ask them 'Do you want to be healed?'(Jn 5:6). Don't straighten me out, I'm enjoying my confusion! While not wishing to underestimate the power of the Spirit, I have met people, and I came away convinced that a personality transplant was what was needed. There was one thing that was certainly needed, and while it is absent, nothing can happen, and that is a sincere desire to be open to all the Lord can do for me. I always find myself going back to a basic requirement, before that could happen, and that is that it is only the Spirit who can create this attitude within my heart. There is no way that I can generate it, or psyche myself into it. It is pure gift, and I can expect to receive it when I'm really ready to do so, and to make use of it. God would never put a desire within my heart without supplying what it takes to fulfil that desire.

Referring back to the seagulls again, the sky's the limit, and I can be as free as I really want to be. To switch the image again, if

I hoist the sails, the wind will move the boat out to sea, and on to the horizon, if that's where I want to go. I really don't think that these images are totally unrealistic, even if I fail to experience this freedom most of the time. There is no way that the seagull will let the wind drive it off course, and bring it somewhere it doesn't want to go. Similarly, with the boat and sails, I do have a rudder, and I can control the direction; as it would be irresponsible to just drift out to sea, and let the wind decide my destiny. When I speak of living and walking in the Spirit as riding the wind, I do not mean that this excuses me from all responsibility, or that I should become some sort of unthinking robotic figure in the hands of a controller. I have to lead my life; I have to make my decisions, and I have to act on those decisions. It is how I approach and handle all of this is what I have in mind here. I am speaking about resigning as a member of the 'white-knuckle' club; of ungritting the teeth, unflexing the muscles, and unclenching the fists. I will get the inspirations, but I must be willing to act on them. The Spirit will give what it takes, but I must provide the body – the hands, the feet, the voice. In the last chapter I spoke about prayer, and how essential it is that I show up. If there's no body, the Spirit has nothing (or nobody) to work on. Grace builds on nature, it doesn't replace it.

Riding the wind is impossible if I'm weighed down with burdens. Some or many of these burdens are imposed on us, and are not self-imposed. However, the Lord fits the back for the burden, and he assures us that we will never be given a burden that is too much for us. Another way of putting this is to have Jesus say, 'I will never lead you where my Spirit will not be with you, to see you through. Nothing will happen to you today that yourself and myself will not be able to deal with.' St Teresa of Avila used to say, 'Teresa on her own can do nothing. Teresa and two ducks can do nothing. Teresa, two ducks, and God can do anything.' For one person something can be a burden, but for the Christian person of faith that same thing can afford an opportunity for growth, and can be a source of blessing. Being a Christian means looking at things from the perspective of Jesus

Christ. 'Who has known the mind of God that he may teach
him? But we have the mind of Christ' (1 Cor 2:16). We can only
surmise what life must look like if we look at it through the eyes
of Jesus. Surely it must be endowed with infinite possibilities.
Eternity is what emerges from time, and infinity is what our
finiteness merges into. In a certain sense, to walk in faith is to
take risks, risks that become less and less so as time goes on.
When the promises of the Lord are found to be reliable and dependable, then the process of trusting comes much easier to us.
It is only when I let go of the bar at the deep end of the swimming pool that I'll discover that I am able to swim. I can hold on
to the bar till the day I die, and I'll never find out if I could swim
or not. For generations, this gamble has paid off, and the simple
fact of that letting go brought on many years of recreation and
enjoyment that would otherwise have been unknown. There is
no knowing all the blessings that will flow from every stepping
out I take. There is a Charles Lingberg within all of us, if we
were just ready to go for it, and discover what is possible. Faith
grows through practising faith; it grows through exercise. I learn
to pray by praying, just as I learned to walk by walking, and to
talk by talking. Of course, the Spirit has a major role to play in
the growth of our faith, but the Spirit cannot become the wind
beneath our wings if we are not prepared to open those wings.

This journey back to the Garden can be an experience of wonder at every turn, if my heart is open to this. 'My God is new
with every new day' is a saying attributed to Cardinal Suenens.
Alice in Wonderland begins her story with these words: 'I could
tell you my story beginning this morning. I couldn't begin yesterday because I was a different person then.' So was I, and so
were you. Catechesis, at best, can be little more than academic
knowledge. Knowing things up in my head is not faith.
Knowing Jesus is God is not faith; even Satan knows that.
Accepting knowledge in my head is nothing more than mental
assent. It is when faith seeps down into my feet, and allows me
step out, that I begin to act in faith. How often have we seen a
parent playing with a child, when the child is thrown into the

air, and caught again, amidst delirious excitement. This is trust at its most obvious. We couldn't imagine a parent stepping back and not catching the child, just to teach it never to trust anybody! The seagull is very familiar with the wind, as is the swan with water. The relationship is a secure one, even though both species had to make that first venture all those years ago. I'm sure the confidence had to grow, until now it is totally automatic. How could I possibly think of my Father being anything but caring, loving, and dependable? Surely, Jesus has done enough to merit our trust, and to receive our confidence. Faith is a response to love. 'There is no fear in love. Perfect love drives away all fear, for fear has to do with punishment; he who fears does not know perfect love' (1 Jn 4:18). To ride the wind is to trust God, and make that leap of faith; something that will change my life utterly and for all time.

# The Pain Barrier

The wall of pain is something that all long distance runners are familiar with. If the marathon is 26 miles long, then, at about 12 miles into it I will hit that pain barrier, and find it really painful to continue. If I were not a trained runner, I could easily drop out at this stage. Because of my training and experience, however, I expect this to happen, and I know that, by just keeping going, the pain will pass, and I will get what is called my 'second wind'. This would be the drop-out point for the novice.

This pain barrier is not confined to long-distance running; it is part of almost everything we undertake in life. There comes a point in whatever I'm doing when the going gets tough, and the temptation to quit becomes quite strong. A recovering alcoholic, with twenty years of contented sobriety behind him will tell you all about the wall of pain, when he very nearly gave up, and stopped trying. Ask any married couple about wakening up some morning, wondering what on earth they've got themselves into. Once again, here is where the quitters quit, because no one told them that this time was bound to arrive, sooner or later. The trained runner, who knows what to expect, can deal with this pain, and will finish the race much fresher than back at that particular part of the race. There is something here for all of us to take on board, if we are to continue on our road back to the Garden. We will all experience those times when, no matter what I have heard about Jesus, and how much I have experienced his loving care, I will be tempted to give in, to compromise, to go for the quick-fix, to risk throwing it all away.

'Have you not learnt anything from the stadium? Many run, but only one gets the prize. Run, therefore, intending to win, as athletes who impose upon themselves a rigorous discipline. Yet for them the wreath is of laurels that wither, while for us, it does not wither. So, then, I run knowing where I go. I box, but not aimlessly in the air. I punish my body, and control it, lest after preaching to others, I myself should be rejected' (1 Cor 9:24-27). In earlier chapters I spoke about the daily dying, the splinters, that are all part of the cross I am asked to carry as part of my life as a Christian. If this came easily and naturally to me there would be very little dying involved. There is a cost in Pentecost. 'Happy are they who dream dreams, and are prepared to pay the price to make those dreams come true' is a statement attributed to Cardinal Suenens. The secret of keeping going is to have some goal in mind, and to keep that before me at all times. 'What a crowd of innumerable witnesses surround us! So let us get rid of every encumbrance, and especially of sin, to persevere in running the race marked out before us. Let us look to Jesus the founder of our faith, who will bring it to completion. For the sake of the joy reserved for him, he endured the cross, scorning the shame, and then sat at the right of the throne of God. Think of Jesus who suffered so many contradictions from evil people, and you will not be discouraged or grow weary' (Heb 12:1-3).

If I keep my eyes fixed on Jesus, I will find what it takes to face up to the pain of following him. Peter stepped out over the side of the boat and, while he kept his eyes fixed on Jesus he could walk on water. As soon as he took his eyes off Jesus, he became conscious of the wind and the waves, he lost his nerve, and began to sink. (Mt 14:22-31). There were times when Jesus hit this pain barrier, and I'm sure, as he prayed all alone on the mountain at night, his soul suffered great anguish. We see a glimpse of this in Gethsemane (Lk 22:39-44). Once Jesus put his hand to the plough, there was no going back (Lk 9:62). He had set his mind on a mission, and he would not let up until that mission was complete. Doing what the Father asked of him was the great driving force in his life.

A group of people set off to climb a mountain. When they get to the foot of the mountain, one section of the group is already tired, and decide not to travel any further. Half-way up the mountain, another section is so touched by the beautiful scenery, that they decide to pitch camp there, have a picnic, and not go any further. The remaining group are very aware that they set out to climb this mountain, and that is what they will do. At the beginning of a marathon everybody runs well, and there's a great air of rivalry and competition in the air. However, it stands to reason that, if I don't finish the race, I don't stand a chance of being reckoned among the winners. It is only they who persevere to the end who will be saved.

I wouldn't pretend to have any great insights into this, but I sometimes think that we can stop too soon in our prayers, and our endeavours to do the good. I'm not particularly hung up on Novenas, if it means that our prayers will be answered only after nine days, and not any sooner. On the other hand, I sometimes think of Mary trying to keep those apostles in that Upper Room for nine days. When nothing was happening after a few days, Peter probably wanted to go home! Thomas wanted proof that something was going to happen or he, too, was quitting! However, the Spirit did come, and he came because he was expected. Mary knew that the Spirit would come, no matter how long they had to wait. I could be praying for something, and the Lord intends giving it to me; but he wants me to grow in trust and confidence, so he may delay in answering, just to see if I continue to pray, and to expect my prayers to be answered. There were times in the gospels where he appeared to be in no hurry to act on something that looked really urgent to others. He knew Lazarus was dying, but he continued what he was doing, and, in the meantime, Lazarus had died (Jn 11:14). Martha had a mild reprimand for him when she said 'Master, if you had been here, my brother would not have died' (Jn 11:21). It was obvious that Jesus knew what he was doing, and why he did it. He was pushing their credulity a little bit, just to strengthen their faith in him. I can well imagine how I could just give up praying for something after a few days and, for all I know, the Lord intended answering my prayer the very next day. I dropped out of the race within sight of the winning post.

In all my reckoning about changing practices, patterns of behaviour, and developing prayer structures and proper living, I
must take into account the very simple fact that a time will come
when my good resolves of now will be severely tested. Like the
Hebrews in the desert, I may yearn to return to the flesh-pots of
Egypt. 'It happened that when Pharoah sent the people away,
God did not lead them through the land of the Philistines, although it was nearer, for God thought that the people might lose
heart if they were faced with the prospect of a battle, and would
return to Egypt' (Ex 13:17). 'The Israelites saw the Egyptians
marching after them: Pharoah was drawing near. They were terrified and cried out to Yahweh ''Were there no tombs in Egypt?
Why have you brought us to the desert to die? What have you
done by bringing us out of Egypt. Isn't this what we said when
we were in Egypt: Let us work for the Egyptians. Far better to
serve Egypt than to die in the desert''.' (Ex 14:10-12).

It is easy to be good on the generalities. I can fully agree that I
should give more time to prayer, to charitable works, to visiting
the sick. The real test of that goodwill, however, is my willingness to mediate that down to the specific. When am I going to
pray? Where am I going to pray? How am I going to pray? What
back-up do I have on those days when that specific time-slot is
not available for prayer? There are many serious questions to be
honestly answered before I am ready to embark on any such endeavours.

I remember some years ago in school, when the new first
years arrived at the beginning of the school year. They nearly all
joined the photography club, the drama group, the outdoor adventure group. Within a month more than half of them had dis-
appeared. By the end of the first term, we were lucky if 20% of
them remained. Once the winter weather set in the Outdoor
Adventure club ceased to be as attractive as it had seemed!
When new films had to be paid for out of limited pocket-money,
or dramatics meant staying in after school ended, the interest in
this activities took a drastic toll on the numbers. If I might coin a
word here, I would use the word stickability. This is possible

only when I am deeply aware of the source of my strength. We are in a constant state of change and evolution. Human nature is not a constant. Only Jesus is the same yesterday, today and always (Heb 13:8). Without his accompaniment, I am likely to grind to a halt and end up sitting on the road, going nowhere.

The Christian way is about being led, and about being accompanied. The young parents are out for a walk with their toddler on a Sunday morning. The child toddles on ahead of them. Now and then he is fascinated by the contents of a shop window. The parents give him time to take in what is seen but, because of a time factor, they may urge him to continue walking. This time he runs on ahead of them, and there is a dangerous intersection coming up, which occasions yet another intervention from them. Then again, as they walk along, he is lagging behind and, when they look back, they discover that he is sitting on the footpath, and has discovered that he can actually scrape any amount of dirt and clay from between the kerb stones. This calls for another intervention, and they're on the road again. After a while, Junior gives up! He's tired, so he just plops himself down on the footpath and is going no further. The parents just pick him up, pop him in the stroller, and continue their walk. If I'm to walk with Jesus, I cannot either run on ahead (into tomorrow's worries), or lag behind (in yesterday's guilt). Jesus will accompany me through every pain barrier if I am prepared to walk with him. I cannot teach a man to walk who won't let go of his crutch; nor can I teach a person to swim who refuses to let go of the bar on the side of the pool.

I mentioned earlier that having a definite goal in sight is a great help in my struggles to get anywhere in life. I know someone who deliberately buys clothes that are too small, so that it provides a target to work towards when the diet begins! Looking at those clothes each day serves as a daily reminder that, if you ever want to wear these clothes, then you know what to do. I must depend, of course, on the Spirit in this whole area of self-motivation. The Spirit reminds us, when we risk losing the vision. The Spirit is a Comforter when the going gets tough.

The apostles were weak human beings, and living with Jesus for three years, listening to him, and watching him in action did very little to change their human condition. It was only after Pentecost that they were set on fire, and went out that door, ready to witness to Jesus all the way to death, if that's what it took. Nothing could ever be the same again, once the Spirit came. I wrote about this earlier in a chapter called 'Popeye's Spinach'. I refer to it here again in the context of that 'stickability' I spoke of earlier. By myself, I just cannot have any kind of reliable predictability. Human nature is very volatile and fickle. Health, age, living conditions, etc., can change the way I see things. Even if the Lord has, on occasions, to pick me up and pop me in the buggy, I'll ask for that if I really want to keep going. Again and again, I repeat my goodwill, hopes, expectations, and good intentions to the Lord. I honestly believe that, when he sees that the sincerity is really there in my heart, he will see me through, and I'll arrive safe and well back in that Garden.

# Life is Fragile

'Life is fragile; handle with prayer.' It has been three months since I wrote that last chapter. I celebrated my 70th birthday in hospital. I had been so 'busy' for the previous few months that my heart told me 'Either you stop, or I stop'! I had no choice but to pull into a pit-stop (Chapter 13), and to give the body a chance to cope with its human limitations. This was a worthwhile experience for me. While I would much prefer to burn out than rust out, I know that I must be prudent and sensible in how I use the body. If I accept that I am a spiritual being in a physical dimension, then, of course, I must give priority to the spiritual. This must never be done at the expense of the physical.

The body is a Temple of the Spirit, a tabernacle, a monstrance, that must be treated with reverence and respect. 'God said, "Let us make man/woman in our image, to our likeness" ... So God created man in his image; in the image of God he created him; male and female he created them. God blessed them ...' (Gen 1:26-27). Strictly speaking, the body is not *me*. I am living in the body. There will come a time when the body will no longer be habitable, and I will have to change residence and go to live elsewhere. Because the body is God's gift, it must be treated with respect, and with care. I can shorten the life of the body by the way I treat it. Like most other things in life, the treatment of the body can swing from one extreme to the other. On the one hand, the body is idolised for its beauty, and the attention and influence such beauty can bring. With the rapid advance of plastic surgery, and implantation, it can become difficult to discern how much of the body is original, and part of God's creation. On the other hand, with drug abuse of every kind, the body can break down, and assume the qualities of old age long before the years have accumulated. Once again, like most things in life, there is a happy medium. Too much of anything is not good.

An earlier form of spirituality tended to see the body as evil, in need of being disciplined, and subjected to submission. It was almost implied that suffering of the body brought blessings to the soul. In those days, one felt as if made of two parts – a soul and a body. They were quite independent of each other, in so far as they had different sources and different destinations. Our bodies we got from our parents, while our souls came directly from God. Our bodies would end up 'a-moulding in the grave', while our souls would 'go marching on', return to God for a detailed check-up, and await the verdict on how my life was spent.

I would no longer accept or proclaim this dichotomy. I think of the soul and body as being eternally entangled, each capable of contributing enormously to the human and eternal welfare of the individual and, at the end of time, the body, which is mortal, will be transformed and given an eternal quality, enabling it to exist in a whole new environment. 'The body is sown in decomposition; it will be raised never more to die. It is sown in humiliation, and it will be raised in glory. They buried it in weakness, but the resurrection shall be with power. When buried it is a natural body, but it will be raised a spiritual body. For there shall be a spiritual body, as there is at present a living body' (1 Cor 15:43-44).

I consider that it is a responsibility we all have as to how we treat the body. As with most things, there's a happy medium. Many of our human ills (sickness) are self-inflicted. Enough alcohol, nicotine, and self-indulgent living, and we cannot blame God if our health is not good. Our minds, spirits, and general well-being, are much enhanced when functioning within a healthy body. A healthy mind in a healthy body. The body is mortal, of course, and there will come a time when it will break down, and come to a halt. In the meantime, however, it is only common sense that I should give it a fair chance; that I should respect this Temple in which God now dwells. At the time of writing, there is no end to the debates and discussions on obesity, lung and liver cancer, and various forms of heart attacks, or heart failures. I honestly believe that I should take responsibility for my own personal contribution to the state of my physical being, be that good or bad.

One area that helps to highlight the important role the body plays in our well-being is the use of the body in prayer. This involves much more than kneeling, standing, or bowing. My inner spirit can express itself in physical ways. As Christians, we can learn a lot about this from other world religions. As I watch the Hindu sitting in the lotus position, back upright, eyes closed, hands laid open; or the Muslim, facing Mecca, and prostrating and bowing, I can see clearly that the body can be involved very directly in prayer. Jesus raised his eyes to heaven, and he lay prostrate on the ground (Mk 14:35). His body was very much involved in his final 'Yes' to the Father on Calvary. Just as a hand can be used to strike, Jesus used his hands to heal and to feed the hungry. He used his voice to teach and to confirm. When he chose to give himself to us, he did so in the form of food and drink, which is received through the body. This must surely highlight the fact that the body is sacred. All kinds of abuse of the body, whether that be physical or sexual abuse, is sacrilegious. It is only when we become aware of the sacredness of the body that we can hope to have any proper level of moral conduct, or ethical values. Because we are rational beings, and can distinguish right from wrong, we are more than mere animal.

I mentioned earlier that many of us inherited a spirituality that implied that the body was evil, and should be punished, and kept under subjection. While this would be no longer accepted, it is important, though, not to throw out the baby with the bath-water. There is a great need to keep the body in check. Our human appetites for food, drink, sex, and other creature comforts, can become tyrannical, compulsive, and addictive, if not kept in check. While these appetites are normal, healthy, and natural, they can run riot if not controlled, and can reap horrific damage to the whole person, and, quite often, to those around. Once again, there is a happy medium; all things in moderation.

Alcohol, sex, food, money, etc., are not evil in themselves. Whether I use or abuse them decides whether they're sources of good or evil. I am speaking of a healthy balance here. Jesus spoke about praying and fasting in the same breath (Mt 6:7, 16). The implication seems to be that by praying, I am nourishing the soul and by fasting, I am disciplining the body. Prayer and fasting seems to be part and parcel of all world religions. I have friends who fast on Fridays, and/or Wednesdays. This is not necessarily abstaining from all food, but limiting one's intake to bread and water, or some such combination. They can very definitely vouch for the fact that this really strengthens their inner spirits. Most of us have experienced the lack of physical or mental energy when we have over-eaten. The opposite happens when we curtail our intake of food. I heard a doctor say that it's the two-thirds extra we eat, that we don't need, that keeps doctors in business.

The general thrust of this book has been our journey back to the Garden. It is significant that when we get there, we will not need our bodies any more. What a tragedy to discover that we indulged the body so much that we lost our souls in the process. All of what I am is entrusted to me by God. I own nothing. I will have to answer for how I used what was entrusted to me. My journey back to the Garden can be greatly shortened through neglect of the body, and not taking responsible care of how I live.

It is not the length of one's life that matters as much as the depth at which it is lived. We are called to be fully human and fully alive. I cannot live life to the full without giving proper care and priority to the body. Some people are physically disabled from birth, and have to live their lives within the limits of their ability. Most people are born in full possession of all their bodily faculties. People in the caring professions make excellent use of their physical abilities in the caring of others. This is seen at its best when laid against the background of those who use the body as an instrument of death and destruction in the lives of others. The hand that plants the bomb, the tongue that tells the lie, the heart that nurses the resentment. To be wholesome (holy?) is to employ *all* that I am in doing good; to make full use of everything God has given me in the service of others. The happiest people on earth are those who give of themselves for the sake of others. When I make myself the centre of my own existence, to the exclusion of others, I am living in solitary confinement, where there is no one else in my life but myself. Selfishness brings a very lonely existence. I have a tongue to speak the kind word, a hand to reach out to others, and ears to share another's burden. I cannot have abundant life unless I involve the body in everything I do. I cannot share abundant life if I have no quality of life myself.

I want to come back to a point I made earlier. In general, it can be said that many people do not pay sufficient attention to their health. Many of the illnesses they inherit are directly the result of a particular lifestyle. The body has an extraordinary capacity to heal itself, if given the opportunity. The body is one of the most intricate of God's creations. People in medicine specialise, e.g. cardiac, orthopaedic, neurology, etc., because no one person could possibly be an expert on all components of the body. It is easy to accept that the inner works of a computer are delicate and complex, as is the engine of a supersonic jet. Imagine someone opening a panel on that computer or that engine, and emptying a bucket of sludge into it. That would be shocking to watch, and it would reasonably be expected that the computer or the engine could no longer function properly. We live in an age where junk food is prevalent, and the body must take ferocious abuse because of the junk that is poured into it. No wonder the body shakes, trembles, sweats, and contorts after being subjected to drugs or to overindulgence of any kind. In my earlier understanding of the creation story, I believed that Adam and Eve were given perfectly healthy bodies and, after the Fall, those bodies became subject to disease and decay. I don't know how true this is, but I do know that I myself have a very real personal say in the level of health and well-being that my body enjoys. I don't wish to generalise too much, because I have known people with throat cancer who never smoked, and people with damaged livers and kidneys who never drank alcohol. The point I am making here is that, in general, each of us must take personal responsibility for our health, and how we take care of the body. I do not believe that this can be isolated from our spiritual life, or our spiritual well-being. Having had several close calls with a damaged heart over the years, I have no hesitation in saying, with hindsight, that all of this could have been avoided. Hindsight, of course, is of no value, apart from the lessons it teaches. I believe it is never too late for God, and a change of the pace and pattern of life can be of great benefit, even when the damage is done. Of course, we will all one day die, but I strongly believe that it is incumbent on me not to hasten the advent of that occasion in any way, and to live life as fully as possible right out to my last breath.

## Hold on to the Vision

During my years of teaching in second-levels schools, I taught Irish, English, Latin, and French. This involved a lot of essay-work, and journalism of different kinds. To instil a very import-ant aspect of essay-writing, I spoke of a chicken drinking water. The chicken takes the water in the beak, and then lifts the head so that the water flows back down the throat. The point I was trying to stress was how important it is, when writing an essay, to lift one's head off the page, and look once again at the title of the essay. It is so easy to wander off the subject, and to get side-tracked into material that has nothing whatever to do with the subject under review. 'Keep your eyes fixed on Jesus, the author and finisher of our faith' (Heb 12:2) is the advice given the early church in the letter to the Hebrews.

In Matthew 14, we are told a story about Peter walking on the water. Jesus came to them walking on the water, and Peter asked if he could do that too. Jesus invited him to walk towards him. Peter did this, and was doing very well until his attention was distracted from Jesus, as he became aware of the wind and the waves. Immediately he began to sink, and cried out for help. Jesus reached out and took him by the hand and brought him to the boat. Every one of us can find ourselves in this situation on many occasions. If we could only keep our eyes, our attention, focused on Jesus, we could experience a whole new power, and a world of infinite possibilities. If, however, we become preoccu-pied with ourselves and our problems, we are in trouble. We change management, and take over the controls ourselves and, of course, this is a recipe for disaster. We cannot manage, con-trol, or run the show ourselves. In the face of life, with all its per-mutations and combinations, we are essentially powerless. We cannot add one moment to our lives, nor can we halt or control the march of time. Despite all the cosmetics and plastic surgery, the aging process is relentless. It is so easy to lose the vision of the reality of human existence. It is so easy to take our eyes off the title at the top of the page, and to get lost in uncharted waters, without rudder, sail, or life-jacket. God has mapped out the road very well for us, if we chose to follow that map. We are on our way back to the Garden, and God sent his own Son to lead us home. We get lost only if we choose to get lost.

In the catechism of my youth we were told that 'Purgatory is a place or state of punishment where some souls suffer for a while before they enter heaven.' Purgatory was not a destination, but something that was part of a journey. While I accept that heaven or the Garden is our ultimate destination, I also like to think of life as being a reality in itself, and not something to be endured while we await something better. In a way, life is an end in itself, because it is during the journey that the graces are received and experienced. There is really nothing I will receive when I get back to the Garden that is not on offer along the journey. I have God, his Spirit, his blessings, and his life. Ok, so I'm 'boxed into' this body and unable to experience all that is available to me. The mystics have no surrounding walls, no horizons, and the third and final stage of life for them will be when the vision is permanent, and all distractions are gone. Saints Thérèse, Padre Pio, etc., struggled in their 'cages' and yearned to fly into the great blue yonder. They were in exile on this earth, but they knew they would make it safely home.

Jesus makes many promises about eternal life. He promises a full restoration of our divine birthright when our present sojourn is completed. 'Anyone who believes in me will have eternal life' (Jn 6:35). 'Those who believe in me, even though they die, will live again' (Jn 11:25). 'Love Story' is a movie that was quite popular some years ago. What was different about it is that the heroine dies at the beginning, and the movie then brings us back through the story that unfolded up to that time. This meant in effect that, as we watched, we already knew the outcome; we knew how it was going to work out. Our lives are something like that. We are asked to live the *now*, and leave *eternity* to God. God doesn't send me anywhere when I die. Rather he eternalises the direction in which I now choose to travel. I have absolutely no concern about the after-life. I am concerned, however, about this present life. My concern comes from the need to ensure that I really live it to the full. All people die, and not everybody lives. Some people settle for existing; drifting along without enthusiasm, wonder, or the sheer excitement of living. They wrap their talents in cloth, and bury them, rather than getting out there in the marketplace and investing all that they are in the wonderful adventure of life. Life can be compared to a lit candle in a dark room, which gives all it has until there's nothing left. It is in giving that we receive. If we do not invest, there can be no return. There is a happy balance to be struck here. While I keep my destiny in mind, and am always mindful where it's all leading, I still give the present moment all I've got. I cannot spend my life sitting around 'waiting for Godot'. The present moment is the sacred moment, and the only time that exists on God's calendar. Just a year or so ago the Olympic Games took place in Athens. I cannot watch an athlete break a world record, or pick up a gold medal, without thinking of all that went before. That medal has been won over the past ten or twelve years, rather than during a ten-second dash today.

Hope is the hallmark of the Christian. Losing hope is the only real sin for someone who is redeemed and saved by Jesus Christ. Jesus has done everything possible and necessary to ensure that we make it safely back to the Garden. Paul tells us that our salvation is based on 'his blood and our faith' (Rom 3:22). Jesus has done his part, he completed the task entrusted to him by the Father. The second part of the equation is whether we hook into that, avail of that, and live with the power that he made available to us. When Jesus had completed the work entrusted to him by the Father, he returned in triumph, to sit at the right hand of the Father. He then sent his Spirit 'to complete his work on earth'. In the second and third chapter of this book, I dealt at some length with the role of the Spirit in our Christian journey. 'Learn to live and to walk in the Spirit', St Paul tells us (Rom 8:9).

The journey is clearly mapped out for us; we are given food for the journey, and we are endowed with all that is needed for a happy and wholesome experience of living life out to the end. Some people seem to get a very raw deal in life; like a poker player with a very poor hand. I don't pretend to understand why this happens to some and not to others. This is something that I must leave until I get all the answers later on. Rilke said that life is a journey from the certainties of callow youth, to a time when we find ourselves living with questions. We learn to live with the questions, and even come to love the questions, knowing that, at some future time, we will come into possession of all the answers. If I were to hazard an explanation, or a possibility, it would be to believe and hope that, no matter what the circumstances and situations of our lives may be, we all have free access to the power of the Spirit to deal with every possible situation life may throw up before us. We have canonised saints from every walk of life, and bearing every possible cross that could happen. St Paul speaks of one of the struggles he experienced. 'Lest I become proud, after so many and extraordinary revelations, I was given a thorn in my flesh, a true messenger of Satan, to slap me in the face. Three times I prayed to the Lord that it leave me, but he answered, "My grace is enough for you; my great strength is revealed in weakness" ' (2 Cor.12:7-9). As it happens I spent most of the past few months in three different hospitals. Thanks be to God for his grace, because I can now fully appreciate the experience as being a wonderful lesson about my own mortality, and the frailty of human existence. I genuinely appreciate all that my experience taught me, and I am much enriched because of it.

Jesus speaks about two men who went up to the Temple to pray (Lk 18:10). One was a Pharisee, the other was a Publican. The Pharisee stood up at the front of the Temple, and began to tell God how good he was, how he had been faithful to all the commandments, and how his life had been a model of perfection. Instead of 'Praise the Lord', his prayer was 'Praise me, Lord.' The other man stood at the back, fell on his knees, struck his breast, and prayed 'Oh, God, be merciful to me a sinner.' Jesus tells us that it is this second man who was justified before the Lord. Those of us who are 'cradle' Christians/Catholics, were placed in the Holy of Holies by our parents and teachers, and the implication was that we should strive earnestly to remain there all our lives. Anyone who followed this literally could easily join with the Pharisee in declaring to God how faithful I have been to every commandment, direction, and instruction of the gospel. Those who have *lived* life will readily admit to brokenness, weakness, and powerlessness, and will have no hesitation in joining the publican at the back, praying 'Oh, God, be merciful to me a sinner.' It is a long journey from the Holy of Holies (where God dwells) to the back of the Temple (where we belong). Holiness involves becoming more and more convinced of my own sinfulness. The nearer I come to God the more obvious my own human weakness becomes. Remember that I am heading back to a warm eternal hug of forgiveness and belonging. The more convinced I am of my need for that the greater that meeting will be.

There is none of us who can claim that we will not, one day, die. Somehow or other, though, there is a tendency to push death back into the background, and not dwell too much on it. This is understandable, and I think it is much healthier to give life all I've got than to be sitting around thinking of dying. We attend funerals, we visit graves, we listen to details of some world tragedy, in which hundreds have perished. We come across a serious road accident, in which some people were killed. I myself discover that, when I move away from such a scene, I tend to drive a little slower, for just a few miles. In no time at all, I'm back to my usual driving, never dreaming that such a thing could happen to me. There is some sort of instinct for survival within all of us that insulates us from direct confrontation with death. We are not sure how to deal with it. Do we face up to it now, or wait till it approaches us? I myself find that the thought of going back home to the Garden gives me a much more positive attitude towards death. On a few occasions during my several periods spent in hospital, I had reason to believe that 'This is it', and I was greatly consoled to discover that the thought did not upset me unduly. I found this to be very reassuring, and I hope and pray that, when the time does come, I will feel then as I have felt on those other occasions. The last book I wrote was called *Jesus said it, and I believe it*, and it contains reflections on 157 promises in the gospels. Many of those speak to us of eternal life. There is no way that I am asked or expected to stagger along on the road of life, and hope to God that it's leading somewhere. Jesus is the Way, and it is only by following him that I can end up in the embrace of the Father. He leaves us in no doubt about this, and he refers to it quite frequently. On many occasions, Jesus referred to the fact that he himself would soon be returning to the Father. This is what kept him going. 'Father, into you hands I commend my spirit' (Lk 23:46) were his final words in death. On several occasions, he reminded the Pharisees that, unlike them, he knew where he came from, and he knew where he was going. St (Padre) Pio said that he would stand at the gate of heaven until the last of his spiritual children entered in. Jesus himself will be there to welcome us, as will his mother, and all of our family and friends who have gone before us. That moment will be a meeting with all our old friends, never having to say goodbye again. Just imagine never having to say goodbye! All of our dreams will be fulfilled; all of our hopes will be realised. Home, home, home at least.

I thank my God that I'm home at last.